The Gestaltbunker

Paul A Green grew up in London. He studied at Trinity College, Oxford and the University of British Columbia, on the MA Creative Writing Programme. He has worked as a radio presenter, teacher, used-book operative and as Lecturer in Media at the Royal National College for the Blind.

His poetry has appeared in magazines ranging from *New Worlds* to *Poetics Journal*, while he has appeared over the decades in pubs, clubs, colleges and festivals, sometimes collaborating with musician Vincent Crane or video artist Jeremy Welsh. Recordings have been broadcast on CBC, WFMU-FM, and Resonance-FM or disseminated online by culturecourt.com.

Plays performed include *The Dream Laboratory* (CBC Radio), *Ritual of the Stifling Air* (BBC Radio 3), *The Voice Collection* (RTE), *The Mouthpiece* (Resonance-FM), *Terminal Poet* (New Theatre Works) and *Babalon* (Travesty Theatre), a celebration of occultist/rocket scientist Jack Parsons. Recent short fiction includes *The Poets of Radial City* in *Unthology 2*, published by Unthank Books. His first novel *The Qliphoth* was published in 2007. A sequel awaits publication.

Also by Paul A Green

Basement Mix
The Slow Ceremony
The Slow Learning

The Qliphoth

Paul A Green

The Gestaltbunker
Selected Poems 1965–2010

Shearsman Books

First published in the United Kingdom in 2012 by
Shearsman Books
50 Westons Hill Drive
Emersons Green
Bristol
BS16 7DF

Shearsman Books Ltd Registered Office
30–31 St. James Place, Mangotsfield, Bristol BS16 9JB
(this address not for correspondence)

www.shearsman.com

ISBN 978-1-84861-193-1

Copyright © Paul A Green, 2012.
The right of Paul Andrew Green to be identified as the author of this work has been asserted by him in accordance with the Copyrights, Designs and Patents Act of 1988.
All rights reserved.

Contents

1. **Directions to the Dead End**
   Aquarius — 11
   The House — 12
   The Time Ship — 13
   The Orange Room — 16
   The Sighting — 17
   The Throne Room — 21
   Caption — 22
   The Destruction of Large Cities — 23
   A Spot in the Oxidised Desert — 26
   Directions to the Dead End — 27
   The Conclusion — 30
   The Gestaltbunker — 31

2. **The Black Museum**
   A Summoning of the Demon of the North — 37
   Catalogue — 38
   A Night at the Black Palace — 39
   The Black Museum — 41

3. **Basement Mix** — 47

4. **Brain Gun**
   Metropolis — 63
   Spontaneous Combustion — 64
   Brain Gun — 66
   Half Light — 68

5. **The Slow Ceremony** — 73

6. **Wapping Rap** — 95

7. **Saxophone Heresies**
   Saxophone Heresies — 101
   Miles Totems Up The Homing Pains — 107
   The Solar Myth Approach — 108
   Dead Letter Blues — 111

8. The Slow Learning	115
9. Brother Paul's Blues	
BP Blues	151
Urban	153
Seething Vacuum Data	155
Dump Cracking	161
Bad Memes	163
Halo	165
Brother 13	166
AJKG 1915–2002	167
Bulletins	168
Brain Stems	169
Thanatron	170
Acknowledgements	173

For Cathy

1

Directions to the Dead End

Aquarius

I'm speaking your fate; so watch the hot valves of this oracle glow. You've paid for these words with bent coins. Galileo arrived on your nativity, but several centuries early. You've often lacked his obstinacy in defiance of the priesthood. Even now in conciliatory moods, you fancy the smells of the confessional—yes, you'd like to admit that the pure inferno of quasars was inhabited by howling angels, who might focus the geometry of their rays, their whole strange benevolence, on your ball of earth, your body of clay, your most unofficial secrets…

But the planet's moved since the morning of your squirming and opening shouts. The bumpy spark-striking dodgems of history were merely Panzers then, are robot bombs now. Some worlds have collided, others haven't. You enjoy making notes but refuse to take part in such star-battles. This will probably kill you.

Moreover—will your cloudy Venus topple out of orbit and lurch into the rings of Saturn, to form yet another halo of debris? Although your lucky tinge is green, your future could be sharp, bloody and glittering as a looted shop front. Or as lumpy as your first baby-food. You try to divine a hard shivering future which is clasped by hot tickling fingers, but your lucky number is the square root of minus-one.

Your fate is as varicose as the Mississippi Delta. Carry that weight, Aquarius.

The House

These beetles rise up on the shiny oiled chain, over the cog on the landing, from the humming boiler room below. All the rooms are served by conveyors. Each beetle measures twelve inches in length.

My grandmother built a rococo altar in the hall. Each of us knelt alone on a narrow strip of carpet. Each strip of carpet was patterned in red. The aspiring Christian crashes upwards, splinters entering his body, as I discovered when the child Jesus intervened in my dreams.

Judas lived in the dining room; he was a waxwork but was capable of propelling himself to my bedside, and his greasy hair hung over me during the night. In the dining room he kept jars. Each jar was five feet in height, rounded at base, made of glazed earthenware.

In my sickbed I would plan flying machines while the snows outside melted or froze. I gazed at the long horizontal beam of the street lamp, yellow on white. I heard the trains, like big bands, in the distance, wailing. I dreamed of my father, floating, wrapped in towels, apparently only nine inches in length on that occasion.

The corridors were polished, although dark. I could not fly down them as I hoped. Their length was uncertain, probably hundreds of yards. Outside it rained or snowed incessantly but the house could only travel in one direction, towards the north.

The Time Ship

The time ship keeps shifting
on the surface of the glass curve
in an eternal parabola
through all strata

under the beds of the fossils
between the crushed artefacts
across the petrified marshes
past the sunken monuments
around the dull red core
(the inflamed red heart of all dreamers)

the bomb-shaped time ship keeps moving into the clay

The captain, permuting his log, a pastime,
sits naked in the control room; a glow
from the master panel; wet blank view ports;
What exists out there? Nobody knows, no

sounds; image scanners outline a grey sun.
Down below: a thickening layer of sand
in the engine room where a tree
has begun to branch. Twigs flex and claw the eggshell roof.

Strands of hair around the bronze terminals,
a scorched switch, bent pins, shattered sockets, dust
swims over relics of rape.
Seminal fluid evaporates,

the first mate's lust became myth
His blinded victim wanders between mirrors, crawls
on corroded catwalks towards the motor cage.
Under the rotors she lies and waits.

All the seeds are dead.

Silence.

Her thighs close.

Glimpses of white limbs (discs spin near her brow)

In the bowels of the ship, the time tree grows.

The warped geometry of dark cabins
contains passengers. Few can remember
their outlines. Some have lost senses.

The Captain crows in his nest.
He is the last member to remember.
He keeps the charts, the maps,
files, tables, crystals, cards, creates the logs…

Giant spools roll through his mind,
holes and gaps gape through his grainy dreams,
time travelogues

again and again
re-reading the book of gnomes
we searched for omens:
there were reports of huge cogs sinking on the horizon

again and again
to re-condition our reflexes
we dissected robots
some protested but tests succeeded

again and again
to revive the old pleasures
we destroyed wide-eyed girls in the smoky enamelled chapel
the soft ashes choked us

TO BEGIN AGAIN/TO FIND A LOST CONTINENT/TO
REFRESH THE SPECIES/TO DISCOVER THE THIRD EYE/TO
GO TO BED WITH ANGELS IN TREES

—was that the clean draft of the manifesto?

I cannot live it
you cannot live it
s/he cannot live it
we cannot live it
they cannot live it

The old terror catches us up in its paw,
the act is ruptured;
as the perpetual shit turns and tumbles on the screen
as the screaming alarms announce time
as the time ship slides and shudders down a rubberised vortex
time flips/over/blinds/my eyes/ are black spots

long gropes

where is the god

where is the man

where are the sibilant guides—our voices—

time drips inside the ship

hollows stone minds

(I am inside the ship)

the ship keeps moving

The Orange Room

The night had come back. The slow vessels were sliding along the distant aqueduct, just visible through the treetops. The waterlogged trees, that splash our windows. The rain is a bad drummer.

In the orange room, the dust had ceased to gather. The atmosphere had begun to glow, like a large cube of quartz. The fire screen concealed a long grey tunnel, paved with moist tiles. From it gusts of air drifted over the long bed. There were hordes of dark balloons hanging in the clouds and a drop of water entered the room. The windows became fragile, under pressure.

You were quite naked in the orange room. There was only a little darkness between our curved spaces. The arc-lamps of the slow vessels patterned our orange walls, while the bottles of the glass genitals began to soften and melt. A spark is discharged between the brass spheres at the foot of the bed. It is often very bright in the orange room.

The Sighting

1. Invisible Aliens Slip Through Our Northern Lights

I am glaring down from 10000 feet
through thin splintered strata of stone-green sky
through split laminations of the ice-green light
through slide after fractured slide of hard air into the snow drift
whiteness is all all light is glazed
light waves and ghosts move more slowly here
I burn with a dry white light I burn a green hole in the sky
I can sift and destroy any grain of snow
it will burn before it arrives at the snowdrift
but I cannot make out the grey mass of my dreams
the yolk that wobbles inside my shadow as my blur grows sharper
Soon I shall fly in my sleep like a floating stone

2. Breaking the Line of the Silence

Bearing down from 2000 feet
the snow has stopped crawling all over this secret wasteland
but even behind smoked lenses my eyes burn
the huge white ledge of the ice age horizon quivers
these motors cannot hold perfect pitch
one overtone can be lethal
over the snow drift
I do not know which machine will design my ghost

3. Beneath the Permafrost Their Entrails Become Artefacts

From here (at 1000 feet) the snow makes no move
under the crust (snow/stone) any deep shelters or caves must be ice-packed
their stalagmite horns point: inwards and downwards

perhaps someone claws through a seam of black blood
under the surface of the drift

perhaps some kind of inhabitant uses this snow
to preserve or compress his dead women

under the weight of the green stones
no one has ever existed perhaps—

a shape steps out of my shadow and moves

the snow makes no move
but this point keeps moving
my blurring dials waver like a single insect
white is the colour of cataract

in the blindness that flares up beneath me
something small and alive is moving

4. The Opal Lights of All Possible Deaths in Her Eyes

Between the vehicle's scorched rim
and a page of snow
there is less than one tenth of an inch

pause

I sit in the infra-red glow of my hot black cell
the starlight makes tiny holes in my hand
footprints are making a final spiral
around the blind side of the hull
towards this cramped blister of one-way glass

a girl's shape steps out of the shadow

between the time-warped plates of this craft
and the stance of her pelvis
sheathed in green leather
seven, eight, six footsteps…

her lips move as she stops
I cannot read her
her fingertips hesitate over her breasts

I am not he who knows
who knows what she is
this new untouchable animal found in the snow

no way I can open the scabbed hatch and go out
only this ship supports my life
my backbone is force-fed with black spinal fluid
as the needle retreats from my scalp one more time

no way she can stumble through the gasping airlock
this ship supports my life only
the young milk that climbs through her platinum spine

might change in this air charged with iron filings

this air filtered through tanks of crushed anthills
this air that changes each second
with the spores that drift from my mouth

between the filaments of her body and mine
between her taut network of atoms and mine
between the spasms between their fragments of light

arc-lights flashing on the high wire grid the high-tension fence that slowly sags
over the edge of our snowbound mass graves

the black thing that is nothing speaks again
as the knife edge of the galaxy turns

as she removes her dark glasses
the snow flares up
as I turn on the strobe in the cabin
her body twists

I look through her eyelids
how can I ask if she sees me watching
the opal lights of all possible deaths in her eyes

5. After the Blackout These Last Readings

I am flying stone-blind in slow orbit: 10,000 feet
the snow falls in shreds for the last time
I am drifting whiteness is all

She is somewhere beneath these heavy stiff sheets
when she sleepwalks into the maze of my cortex
she does not undress

for I unidentified flying observer
must grope out of flight trance
at random but frequent moments
to find the same pattern still fading on the screen
the lines of force that flow through her solar plexus
flex steadily towards the north

it is time to retreat through the tunnel of sub-space

to return to my home built black planet

to retire to my sinking black palace
to record this last rite

I play myself back into darkness

The Throne Room

The throne room can be found beneath the city surface, an octagonal chamber at the intersection of eight tunnels. The floor, walls and low flat ceiling are all plated in heavy sheet iron, patterned by a large but finite number of rivet heads.

The sources of light are outside the room, somewhere in the tubular tunnels diffused, diffracted, perhaps. A dusty glow, faint and red, intrudes from the mouth of each tunnel. Narrow slots traverse the floor. They run from the eight dim openings and cross at the throne room's centre on a small rusting turntable, which does not appear to move, yet slowly and noiselessly turns, clockwise. At the time of writing, this imperceptible movement is the only activity in the throne room.

In the mouth of the north-west tunnel, a throne is stationary. It is probably no longer in use, for the rich upholstery is stained and slashed, chrome has peeled from the bumper around its base, and the panels of the high back are buckled and scratched. Yet cables still festoon the canopy and hang in clusters from the spiked skullcap. It is vacant. Few have glimpsed an occupied throne, either in motion or at rest.

A smell of scorched rubber enters the air. The studded walls vibrate. From the north and east, a rumble of approaching thrones.

Caption

This is the City of Worn Tablets. Over the centuries, the writings engraved on these stones have been worn away by anxious fingers, curious thumbs and the pressure of lips. Once every cornerstone and lintel of this citadel was intricately patterned, with pictographs, runes, ideograms, characters of every kind. The masons never paused in their craft, inheriting as they did a holy function, the creation of an incessant poem for the dead. They were often interred inside awkwardly shaped niches or chambers that were hollowed behind their handiwork, together with small bronze tubes or "fire-cylinders". Those may have been used to transmit short bursts of pyrotechnics, and coloured fire-signals of this kind may have held the universal code to all their doom-signs.

The Master Craftsmen had the privilege of interring themselves. Faint soot marks can be observed in one of the most remote and crooked chambers, deep in the basements of the City. It is remarkable, too, for the elaborate fury of its workmanship.

But the long rains came, followed by tornadoes of ash and pumice. And then, after rolling waves of insectoid life, violent electrical storms, which fractured the City's huge protective dome. Exodus must have followed, and interbreeding of the surviving inhabitants produced only dwindling generations of vandals. So total was the self-destruction that we have no clear idea of the physiology of the inhabitants, only a jumble of charred bones.

The Destruction of Large Cities

IN THAT DRONING CITY (THE NEST)

each vox is a fuzz box

dead centre point

where the young insects feed
in the mouths of the ancients
whose masks smile and scream
dead silently

and I am trying
(come closer my love)
to talk gently

IN HELL THERE ARE NO ECHOES

footsteps stop
outside the door
where no switches exist
for breaking the circuit of the systems of lighting
(and power)

there is only a hand
on the handle

there are no echoes

stop

do not be hysterical

WAR GAME

playground frozen

white on black

flash

scorches bulb ice hot

blind men lead blind children
(slow motion)
in wavering circles past a scorched flag

ring dem bells

UNDERNEATH THE BLACK PLANETS

(revolving, invisible)

doom city exists
lost citadel crushed by the counter-attack of the forests

near one broken dome
stained skull, opening slowly to the sky
(vegetation has crossed the perimeter)

she waits for me

I come each night
with a fresh mutation of flowers

cannot console her

FINAL NEWS HEADLINES

on the fifth side of the empty war room
we found the tapes still running
(machinery survives intact below the surface)

SURVIVE/SURVIVE/PROTECT/SURVIVE/DO YOU COPY?/
IT'S TOTAL/OK U.K./HER AGONY/MAGGOT TALKS/USA

DEAD CHIEFS PEACE PIPE MISSION/QUEEN CONFESSES/
RAYGUN OVERAWES THOSE GAYS/KEEP CRUISING BABY/IT'S
TOTAL/BABY GUERILLA KILLER/BURN UP/GOLD MENACE/
GOLD BLOCK/THE YOLK OVERFLOWS/HOB'S LANE RAPE/
PRESSURE INCREASES/PLEASURE DROME HORROR/
IT'S SENSATIONAL/SHELTER GIRLS/ALL SYSTEMS GONE
PINK/WHITE OUT/GROUND ZERO APPROACHING/KING
KONG BORN AGAIN /OPERATION GOD HITS OUT/WAR IS
LAXATIVE//WAR IS LAXATIVE/WAR IS LAXATIVE/TERMINAL
ZONE CONTACT/DO YOU READ ME FAT MAN?/HOT DAMN
GONNA BUST MY GUT/IT'S BREEDING SUN POWER/STAR
POWER/SUN POWER/

**BURN BABY/BURN BABY/BURN BABY BABY/BURN BABY/
BURN BABY/BURN BABY/BURN BABY/BURN BABY/BURN
BABY/BURN BABY/BURN BABY/BURN BABY/BURN BABY/
BURN BABY/BURN BABY/BURN BABY/BURN BABY/BURN
BABY/BURN BABY/BURN BABY/BURN BABY/BURN BABY/
BURN BABY/BURN BABY/BURN BABY/BURN BABY/BURN
BABY/BURN BABY/BURN BABY/BURN BABY/BURN BABY/
BURN BABY/BURN BABY/BURN BABY/BURN BABY/BURN
BABY/BURN BABY/BURN BABY/BURN BABY/BURN BABY/
BURN BABY/BURN**

A Spot in the Oxidised Desert

My armoured brain reverses through sepia dreamscapes; brown light breaks in through slits in my blistered mask. The shuddering gearshift is probably locked in reverse—I can still sense the slow motion of my scorched shell, the odometer whirling me backward through the rusty haze, while the blue fumes on my breath leave soot on the dashboard.

In retreat, everything changes.

The blur of letters on the inside of my turret are now cryptograms. Last orders and prayers can be safely mouthed backward. The caterpillar tracks cover the same ground, meshing firmly in ruts of fused sand. A clump of molten signposts comes into focus.

There are thousands of thin red lines scored on the flanks of the dunes but veins do not pattern this desert. My vessel crawls into the bed of a shallow canal, on a pavement of crushed prosthetic limbs. (A foot or a hand still occasionally flickers).

Then trails of intricate rubble intercept. The oasis. At this spot, an enlarged insect might collapse beneath its own weight. On reaching this point, the whirring carpets
of enemy spiders would revert to wild, run wild. From a small but typical, tilted maypole hominid relics swing in a bag of webbing.

The ornithoptric men crashed in their thousands.

At this point the windscreen begins to shiver. Soon all my components will start to vibrate at the same frequency.

Before us, the desert is cobbled with stahlhelms.

Directions to the Dead End

1

Be prudent:
This planet has a beginning,
a middle and an end.

At the dead end, dismount.
Walk through the burying ground; touch
the mound at the base.

Look up at the tower, the grid, the silvery hairy antennae.
Watch the panel on the plinth,
the dials, the frozen meters, the icicle spiders
reach solid state.
The absolute is zero.
Perfect machines contain no moving parts.

2

Do not panic, do not be pagan. Be prudent. Avoid convulsions. Hear these instructions. You must not forget you are approaching the dead end. There will be no more signals. Follow our signs. The handrails are provided for your own protection. Remain on the path. Avoid spoors. Do not be disturbed by your guides. They are there to help you across the final meters of the midnight zone. Abstain from beans. Do not remove your masks. The guides will intone your names when the time comes. Do not remove your gloves. They will be specially treated for the final handshake. Do not expose yourselves. Do not accept any immodest songs, books or pictures that might be offered to you at the wayside. Protect your nervous system. At the dead end, on the ledge of the dead end,

STAND BACK

The slim end of the shining edge is hardened, serrated, live.

3

I arrived at the dead end several days ago

after many evolutions
after ritual purifications
after stamping out my birth mark
after slicing out my tumours
after smoking out my nest of serpents
after hammering my shadow
after burning down my shadows
after cutting up my writing
after breaking my assemblies
after erasing my warped tapes
after distilling my bodily fluids
after savaging my dogs
after draining off my cesspit and smashing the sump
after smashing my crutch and cane
after scouring my fleshpots
after strafing my floodlit bed
after testing my gold guardians (chuckling in sulphuric acid)
after tickling my clown to death
after strangling my private puppet
after stuffing my corpses with fuel-soaked rags
after digging my own cave
after flooding my charred ark
after the purgative flood
after human sacrifice

I came to the dead end

three thousand light years from the Vatican
where all the parallels converge

4

Infinity is dotted with rotating corpses…
their domed helmets sparkle, their tangled lifelines
unroll from concave bellies

and particles of an enormous query
jerk through their barbed electric fibres

The transmitter floats a few feet away
from the rim of the dead end.
It is spherical, compact and far too small.

The Conclusion

The square has been disused for a decade. The stone beasts, concave fountains on cracked pedestals, the crooked fractured bollards—all buried beneath a layer of fine grey snow. Grains of grey snow have been falling for months. Visibility is poor.

We have started clearing the central piazza with heavy earth-moving equipment and the customary napalm jets. The men have complained about the unusually mucous snow which furs the windscreen blades and seeps into their cabins, or clogs their valve controls. They've also been disturbed by the findings in the strata below the snow-face.

Apart from wrecked street furnishings, crushed dentures and shards of bone, they've encountered lumps of deep-frozen tissue speckled with metal fragments and curious flattened rubbery objects, like inflatable insects. These surfaces are also treacherous. A flame-thrower operator lost his footing, with unfortunate results.

But I have ordered the men to wipe their visors and trudge on. I have no choice. Visibility is poor. One must not lose control.

Our main objective must still be locating the Chambers. The Chambers offer ascent. They encapsulate a kind of salvation.

I keep telling the men, the wretched lumpen men in their barely protective uniforms, what we are looking for. "They're like booths," I shout. "Cylindrical. About two to three metres high. Domed. Finished in a dark marble-like material…" The men look for humps in the grey snow. I look for transcendence. A conclusion.

The Gestaltbunker

In this deep shelter
(a converted washroom)
the furniture of survival
sustains me

I can work here
wrapped in damp polythene sheeting
only loosely strapped
to my cold cracked throne

I can write my last name
on the tiles
in dandruff

Left alone
I can fumble
with the four last things

NUTRITION
that tooth-pocked hose on the faucet
is flooding my palate with dregs of plankton

the world is eating the sum of its parts

INPUT
the grey-green egg of a cathode tube
keeps me informed and well-lit
with the dazzling striped light of the weltschmerz

the airwaves will soon resume normal shape

OUTPUT
the keyboard of the teleprinter
satisfies my tactile itch

each word jerks off   into the void

I'm a poltergeist   with a bren gun

EXCRETION

I'm seated at the end of the food chain
on the site of the earth's last closet
after the labyrinth of jaws and colons
a soil pipe down to the Silurian

MY SPECULATIONS ARE VERY LOUD

Can I shield my sex with plywood
from the oily feathers of the Venus Flytrap?

Can I smell out my own body
before the nerve gas tickles my septum?

How can I hear the music of the fleas
and a few trees strumming in the whirlwind
before the firestorm melts these lead walls?

I TELEX THIS MEMORANDUM:

the smudged drum of the printer unrolls:
this is the whole picture

INSIDE PASSIONATE GNOME'S HATE NEST WE DECODE
PAPA DADA/TALK   TALKS ON HI-JACKED SEX PLANE PLAN/
FILTH TEENS TRIBE FEST/
GOLEM SURVEY FOOD FREAKS KILL/FOOD KILLS/ANTHRAX
PILLS
KILL/ MUD MURDER RAPE RAP/RIP'n'REAP/MIZZ PIG IS TUFF
TITTY/
DEATH FREEZER/COPS NAB VD KING/CZAR DOOM STRIKES
STAR/

DEATH SUMMIT LOVE/GARBAGE STRIKE DEADLOCKS/"THE
FOOD KILLS"/ CIRCUIT NOISE/CLEAR CIRCUIT /J EDGAR
BEAVER ORGY POLICE RIOT

"TOO MANY WRONG FISH IN THE SEA" /RIOT FREUDS ROT
WRIT UNCLEAR
FBI NIX IRA DNA NIX ON IRAN AND GB/KGB DNA

protein police food slayings/security masks death public issue

DEAD   AIR   DEAD   AIR
DEAD   AIR   DEAD   AIR

I type 4 letters with 1 finger

far below
in the depths
of the plumbing
a choked spasm

first blood
then water
brims over
the bowl

morsels of underwear, dental plates
the sooty filter of a gas mask
a contraceptive bulging with tobacco
the pulp of a thousand oil-smeared publications
dance on the spume of the dark liquid rush

before I die, floating downwards
on the quiet waters of this septic tank
I'll at least be certain of the time
on the kidneys of the protein clock
on the golden brown crystals gather and thicken

IT IS NOW THE HOUR OF THE GREAT CONTEMPT

2

The Black Museum

A Summoning of the Demon of the North

I have been seated for some hours at my onyx altar, which has been specially equipped for writing. It is late November and thin ice is already forming on the bronze tureen of secret fluid, which sits in its crucial place at the alcove in the North Wall. As prescribed, the temple is bare, but the miserable rites are failing.

I am undeniably facing North yet I feel nothing. The rear-view mirror on my altar is frosted with sparkling cracks. I can clearly see nothing.

Perhaps a tall man could be standing behind me, slightly to the left. He may well be wearing conventional garb: black evening suit, stiff white shirt, black shoes, white gloves, inevitable dark glasses and a touch of rouge. I do not wish to confirm my suspicions by turning, but I turn down the light.

I am not ready. And I have no questions. Yet already there are indistinct answers; which gently increase in volume. Perhaps he is using a megaphone or bull-horn. Indeed, there is a metal-rimmed cone of darkness behind me. And I sense an albino sparrow in the room.

Then larger, more predatory birds, pillow after cold ruptured pillow of feathers and wings, gulls, hawks, maybe a small whitish vulture, a flurry of unfolding wings (from the mouth of the bull-horn?) and everywhere now on the altar cloth—white droppings, frozen droppings.

The mad birds seethe on all four walls. It is snowing heavily here. The snow man has drunk all my secret fluid. He must be gaining incredible density. I am impressed, very impressed with his tricks. He must have been impressed with mine. But soon I shall grasp his deafening mumble, soon he will understand my speech, for the opening syllable of his name fills my mouth, I have his name:

he is/ I am

AMAYMON AMAYMON AMAYMON

Catalogue

In the last analysis

>   all symbols can run backwards
>   the missiles stiff with mud
>   sink slowly in their watering holes

In the last analysis

>   we are all prophets
>   Noah's houseboat wallows through the wine-dark sea
>   the flywheels of the maelstrom gather speed

In the last analysis

>   behind the airtight confessional door
>   get ready to chop up your women
>   when the priest opens his ironclad belly

In the last analysis

>   we shall all fall asleep end to end
>   on the trembling couches of amniotic plush
>   (the red couch expands—I grow small and dark)

In the last analysis

>   we crawl through the bricked-up warrens
>   past frescoes depicting the Lives of the Rats
>   while the world's sewers are brought into close
>   alignment

In the last analysis

>   when the desert rumbles through a sieve
>   I am busy decoding my neural pulses
>   while the flames run about in the dwarf-light.

A Night at the Black Palace

Tonight all ritual returns and circulates
Tonight we resume the moon games, for one night only
the bulbous lights of numerous moons assault us

Room within room trembles in orgy
as the gothic bath-house seethes with nymphs
and all our forked beasts are tuned

OUR DEPTHS ARE FULL OF SOUND

The churning propeller of the submarine organ
agitates in compressed air
and the thin petals and blades on particular saxophones
are, at this time, hot and transparent

The glass walls of each cubicle
are stained and cracked by incessant drumfire…

OUTSIDE, IN THE HEDGEROWS OF SMOULDERING
      GREY HAIR
THE SCREAM OF A WHITE FROG

Behind my eyes the cross-hairs are taut
The vulcanised princess swims in her trough
Above her, rotating on spits
large segments of oozing fruit or meat
a small blue flame hovers by her nipple

The molecules of a breast dissolve in wine
The level of liquid in the trough rises—unlace the nets that restrain us
The voices of the ghosts must be rising in pitch
This fruit must be smashed by morning

Tonight, in our last series of talks
we are shrived in the church of the black rock
on the sharpened black crystal rock hard altar

This sacrament is lucid
Our sins are subtracted on the black abacus
The sermon is preached through the black megaphone
(black megaphone)

You are lifted gleaming from the dark trough by the goggled and masked musicians
(each carries a black lacquered saxophone)

The heavy wings are lifted to my shoulders
shrouding my body as it rises in the dark vault…

Harden the lining in your red mouth
I am flying astride a darkened bomb

above the valley of your black lily

The Black Museum

My old age
survives my ice age

in this cryogenic cell, my dead egg,
where my stiff self has exhibited his torso
for a number of crystalline seconds (wax aeons?)

in this black-domed museum,
my ex-mausoleum.

The rhyming clocks have stuck
in the hall of fame.

Their silence signals my liquefaction,
as gas giggles again in my gut,
while an eye bubbles softly in its steaming crater,
and my iced cage defrosts in a flood of blonde light
the seconds dribble afresh through my gristly heart

… I yawn
—these resurrections are turgid,
but that long peristaltic worm of the dream
can stretch my rigor mortis no further.

Muzak flushes discretely around me;
(the senses are making a judicious come-back,
I disinter them with care,
they wear grey).

The Museum swirls and settles around me;
(after centuries, the right cue:

The Curator selects his seal of survival,
in turn, he returns to the Dioramas)

There were no clues in my sleep,
just a mumbling shroud.

There were no blues on my astral travels,
only the bad seven-handed boogie
rolling and tumbling on the spider man's keyboard.

There was no news in my black-out
but bad news: a giant dwarf
is at large in the cosmos.

There were no innuendos in my visions;
merely the hollow scream of an android,
her buttocks tortured in a web of black nylon
while from (concealed) wailing wells the warbling oil
overflowed the slim font in the nave of her ghetto grotto
at my command.

There were no allusions in my trances,
simply a reference I still can't trace:

like the vast dirigible bulk of God,
the Black Museum swims through the abyss

Those dream directives outline my future:

my old rope knotted with nibbled femurs,
my worn shaking pipeline of silver bullets,
my frayed hose fouled with electric eels,
my ancient extruded intestinal snail,
my venerable treacly umbilical serpent—
that inches its slow tangled weight through each dusty archway
towards a winch at the sacred pithead
of the savoury midden I channel within me
that secretes (inside me) retrievable secrets:
the shrouds of monoliths
the flesh of pyramids
a Tibetan book of mortuary cosmetics
God's pointed hat
his luminous nose
a banqueting table once graced by harpies
the wrist of an almost perfect lead woman

the Fuehrer's Tarnhelm
the bottled oracle of Panurge
my shrivelled grey apeskin bag of soul crackers
a vulgar gold-plated coprolite
the Wolfman's mohair suit
Count Dracula's tapered silver boots
a monocle abandoned at the centre of the earth
the Stone of the Philosophers
a plaster model of the Smaragdine Tablet
a sedan chair used by Barabbas
the indestructible food of my Golem
a clock that exploded in the midnight hour
a rusty capsule of an unclaimed time-ship

the Abyss and its daemon Choronzon
an abbess and her corpulent demon Glasybolas

a succubus writhing in a white lace shift
her sisters in the flaming robes of their Klan
a dollar bill smeared with their menstrual blood
the skull of a squashed cat gorged on goats' kidneys
a well-armed tabernacle
a cold brain purchased on the black market
the rugby songs of Valhalla (on vinyl)
my ancestors' rag-time death-march (on wax)
the half-molten trigger of a ruined ghost-trap
forged tickets for the Day of Wrath
the limpid hull of a young girl's spacecraft
its cargo of hair-nets and blood-stained mirrors
a saxophone bearing an ancient curse
the dark glasses of the High Priest
the world's roaches in perpetual motion
finger-prints of the walking dead
all your obituaries and babelgrams
all my unedited unopened letters
the foxtrotting spider I have trained to draft them
the drunken dragon that prefers to burn them
the eraser that rubs out human filth
the back-firing death ray that's strapped between our legs

a black uncut book of new Alephs
this revised catalogue of dark arcana
and the word, which mouthed backwards unmakes the cosmos
ad infinitum etc.

I, curator, catalogue-maker,
am sole exhibit in this Black Museum.
I shall soon clatter through the empty halls,
through renewed old ages, past the dark glass cases,
down the long balustrades, through the blank chambers,
down misty cloisters, around hollow pillars, running
through the vacant hallways
trying to invert the word, and its small black noises.

3

Basement Mix

Basement Mix

this needed RE WRITING

"crumpled chill"

this needed re-writing, overwrought: "the inaudible
whistle of silence"
(dub: great black smear down all walls)

ripple it up
and over the frame OVERWROUGHT

"furry with erasures " (fury)

I'm still ready for cramming
the cannibalised remixes
down and down

"stark bleeding animal skin"
into the crumbs of erasures
red oxide dust

TAKE 1

began the first primal scrawl (squiggle/squawk) on the
matted floor of old William's flat

a calligraphy of my sly hopes
(growing/growling inaudibly)

those long lines

diagrams of flow

breaking their boxes

already ready for cramming engrams

TAKE 2

began first scribble
this quivering ventriloqual feedback:
"It's been the ruin of many a young man…"

TAKE 3

began scratching text three five seven years ago

(back brain up to its old tricks:
"Why Satan is a tit man"
pretend not to look
when you're peeping in the shop front)

biro looping into lewd fuddles

TAKE 4

began "going pink" brain turning
green darkness returning
around the candlelight
walls turning in
into lairs of graffiti

in the dark

I trundled out my droppings: "crumpled chill of a
purple quilt the inaudible whistle of silence great
black smears down the walls all I've left behind black
smears"

against a black ground of basement white

TAKE 5

began with grunts
the Pentel skedaddled
across bumps of a page
candles trembled in slim bony holders
the flea died in a sofa
to the thud of speaking magnetic cones
yet ladies and gentlemen in all dark corners of the universe
my speech was yet incomplete
speech

TAKE 6

began flattening a curling A4
letters looming their projections
of my old tack tack tat
(lugubrious game)

"the wanker is very cramped"

in this basement game where I am being kept
dark as mushrooms in the damp-room

the bog needed dyno-rodding

TAKE 7

began basement tapes: cue the sax
and old words old words
"upstairs a smashed sitar"
tape loops, pools old noises
hoots of potty yowlings
"how can I hear you hearing me
howling that immense long-distance call…"

TAKE 8

began here/any number would do/one can stop dead/here do
dreams hold the answer—they smell intimate enough or
is that random automated trivia retrieval? or the old
wet spurt in the desert?

UNSCRAMBLE THIS: This is a snake… quite small. Small
whitish scaly head—which diverges. Into two (2)
bodies. Twin little tails. Thrashing through low brick
archways. In and out of darkness. It is a protected
species, nothing to do with this business of trying to
live in two places. here and there. His and hers.

TAKE 9

began coming closer, the old words: "Here are a few
words I've picked out of my pocket at random for the
millions of local visiting universes/why can't I turn my
brain down to hear one under-developed child's crooked
syllable?"

but curvatures of bronze, ligatures cramp bites of wood
to cry chaos beyond any old phonemes
through cosmic white trash hiss
old brain

TAKE 10

the knowledge: what my brain's folded/can it/ my highest
itness/ "overblown by leathery farts and the crackle of
damned men's breakfasts" thunder through the astral
webs, and who can hear that drone slow, slyly back thru
cosmic white mush fizz, and has William of the Woollen Hat
rumbled that curry full of old age mysteries, the World
God's electroencelegraphy?

and does moonlight entrance cold waters
and have I gutted my queasy mysteries?

please sir/madam—what animal do we live in?

TAKE 11

outside the speckled window
church gongs time tremors
through a whole pearly sky
that won't need me to milk it

and pink wet hydrangeas
carrying on

TAKE 12

"Upstairs Captain Bee Fart drools ferociously on vocals, harmonica and soprano sax. He has true grits. The Captain has a mouthful of gristly, bitter food that he is trying heroically to eliminate." There was sunlight on the red brick wall and its breed of nettles. The first clouds of autumn.

TAKE 13

stones raining
on the plateau

but they fall to eye level
before the fall

and in the forest of nettles
and disused bedding
a typewriter steadily rusts

naturally some of these birds were insects
and how my psychedelic shack
rises on twisted stilts

but if the spheres flutter
into configuration
attract/repulse/attract

and she who will be you
will be shouting

storm time

TAKE 14

Hearing a child's thinning cry. And the marbles of
logos, ontology, epistemology, all that's crash landed us.
I should have stood up, rolled up all those bad poems
with their instamatic gawp, down the hole of the whole.
And then washed my mouth out. Because I was still stuck,
the old words worm-holing out from the past, struck down
by blots of light. So I walked around myself.

Program wouldn't cancel.

TAKE 15

But the scrawl of every night was unique, like the
patterns of dirt on the carpet, the alignment of tatters
of dirty paper. "This blind pressure, slower, slower,
there's a rush on. Midges. Or mad sperm, rushing
upstream upside their floating metaphysical side
show…"

I am who is at the delta bottle-neck, bending,
straining, grabbing for the true note

want bright lights

wanna rock in the same old boat

TAKE 16

"There is no writing"

The writing on the wall:

"bared her breasts slowly, nipples brush palms lightly.
The hardening…"

I am keeping my tomb shut

TAKE 17

We sleep in order to protect ourselves
domestic difficulties, beyond any word-play

or self-help porno: "Pulled down her pants…
bounce them around," but no solution

while taboos drop away like tarnished sequins

"I'd savage any ice box
for a drop of young golden blood!"

TAKE 18

Backhand smell

watch ticks

to the rhythm of red lozenges

lumps of me hang everywhere

the therapy gun is a scattering machine

I am a lump

in the hot seat

in the red sky

SURVIVE SURVIVE SURVIVE

TAKE 19

one has to be one has to be
one has to be one has to be

to survive the splitting seconds of last night's cathodes
the glassy walls of what is unreturnable

mutating in the body alone
brain-powered meat ready for the licking

one has to be one has to be
one has to be one has to be

but the house was tidy at my final departure
I had to make a coherent exit

TAKE 20

I had left my wife. I was living in that basement. The words had taken themselves into care. There were voices. Upstairs Captain Bee Fart heroically eliminates harmonica gristle. The writer/landlord upstairs did a thump dance all over his Olivetti. I was trying to overdub an endless recursion of white rooms. Sock smell. Sheet crinkle: "Crumbling chill."

It broke up in comix, jags of dialogue. All I've left.
Tharg rules, we are all aliens, all plural presences.
Huge black smears down the walls. Phlegmatic sax
bleatings.

In hibernation, in my teddy bear sweater, tentacles
stung. "That was the aria of the underground policeman,
proceeding through swing doors on the weather-house of
Venus." Collectively conspiratorial automata walk at
the pace of precariously carried mirrors, as deadly as
the virgins of Delvaux, sent out to move in chilly
processions through the green velvety night.

"Extrusion of my sticky lust-numbed body space!"

The ghostly spiral of sex noises overdubs more subtle
brain events.

TAKE 21

Imagine: a sheep. A robot sheep, lost in the fog.
Imagine: the smell of cooking. Imagine giving up
smoking. The pie catches fire and burns out the cooker.

TAKE 22

Clouds shine through my back door
beyond a dirty grimace
imaged through streaky glass:

time tremors
younger hydrangeas
damned mysterious flowers

aircraft dopplers away
again and again the old tale
fading out

TAKE 23

WORD SALADS YOU CAN PAY TO IMPROVE

Frost-fried Hannibal naturally titivates those elephantine nights. But there aren't enough rocket men to go round for my kind of night-porterage. Norse virgins with the order of the silver cross shape some unusual molecules, when placed subcutaneously in the drugged body. Astrally, it's best to be sky-high to a dandelion. Keep the glottal stops. Summer afternoon rays only decode through stained glass. I have seen it in the eyes of old aunts who focus the secret spectra into a tiny image of the Hindenburg:

"Thousands burned in the air…"

TAKE 24

whisky and a sore throat
drizzle in Marylebone

this grouping; a bare rhythm
vexing as light burning

underneath the carpet
where trashmen find sleeping insects

as sun balls through the milk round
humanoids in rout
remember witch doctors

escaping burning krals

TAKE 25

this detention for thousands of lines
time to bend over the keyboard

I kept my mouth cleaned wide open
to swallow November stars

yes mate the need for soft junctions
and a pipeline of burning honey

this checkpoint overnight
when the cells turn round

to start walking home

TAKE 26

I'd had a small furtive underground breakdown in the
summer of 77, that was all. This was my data base,
before I began playing with it.

Beyond my micro-squalor, malnutrition killed off
millions anonymously. Soviet cosmonauts were an
endangered species, and somewhere in Birmingham an old
man was burned alive, an old woman starved to death.
That was all old words. Just a false tooth, in high vacuum.

TAKE 27

Cue the blue, the long donging horn.

Mix into separations of half-light, overlays.

TAKE 28

groping through all the silences
waiting for one that's all clear

here I can see/hear
through hiss and dribble

the gobbing mob
I've sold on

yet as soon as silence is touched
I'm filling it

with reel-to-reel private soul radio
sax ectoplasm baby

stream of blue-green orgone tracers
go flying with the flow

cruise missiles nosing through night
loop the old script in hi-fi

the time's shrinking while you hunt your head

TAKE 29

Those sparkly flashbacks, griping me in raw stomaching,
were the side effects of the upstairs rescue mission.
"Things are quite out of control below stairs, he has
not hit bottom yet, nor contracted a reliable psychosis!"

I was pacing in tiny circles in the smallish tatty white
room. The tape machines sang, "Go, Johnny, go!" and I
sang it for drinks on Friday, Saturdays, and Sundays.

My homegrowing hypnotherapy was a memoire of smudged
dreaming, mostly in locked mirror cabinet settings,
which I had just invented as an escapologist's metaphor
for sex/money anxieties, self-inflicted knowbot
malfunctionings.

Muscular tremors worried me at first but faded out after
reading Nietzsche.

Got the taste for saxophone heresies. I was as grubby as warm plasticine in the grey sheets, but teetered out every night craving impossible relationships.

"The hysterectomy of laughter reveals the red slugs of pain doing their roadwork..."

TAKE 30

In the basement
in the half-light dancing to my shadows
in the furry yuck Pooh bear sweater

I and (I) and ((I))

toasted through this version of the noises about things

beyond the rings of Saturn

Perfect revision? I'd need a brain dump
I became totalled
a write-up

that's all there was

let's go let go

4

Brain Gun

Metropolis

another diplomat hangs himself to swing slowly
like a briefcase bulging with small burnt sins

tear gas gets the gut going
eardrums of mob rage is shaking me hollow

—into total dyslexia that's my last style
we're at the twilight of mannerism

the grammar stammering "he goes" into silence
I'm at the fine frills of disintegration

like police/fire/ambulance only an answering surface
and dirty white riot in surgical wards

the dirty white rot sets/in deep freeze/frame:
THESE ARE ESSENTIAL MESSAGES

crisp desperate radio vowels (police/fire) are sub-titled by my droodles
I draw the sign EAT/DIE but recall the Luftwaffe: "Britain can take it"

the English drinking in their "pubs" through a rich smog and the red
glare of bomb scares
every one is wearing/has worn out their synthetic tissues

THE PLEASURE CORE MODULE IS COMPULSORILY BATTLE-
HARDENED
happy dada is this old loser who is "booze"-mad at the storming centre,

is

Spontaneous Combustion: A Précis

Witness an extraordinary and gruesome phenomenon, spontaneous combustion, in which a person's body is reduced, within minutes to a heap of cinders. No case exactly like another... some of the usual features, according to brown-and-white graphs, neat graphics, black/white photographs released by the Authorities, are the speed and intensity of the process, often associated with an oily smoke, "somewhat sweet like starting a new oil-burning central heating system" a mystifying kind of fuel which cannot be extinguished by water, the way it is selectively directed, for example, leaving the extremities of the body unharmed, sometimes not even damaging the clothes encasing the body.

Examples: sole remnant of Dr John Bentley (1966), "the lower part of his right leg browned by the heat, the shoe still intact"; the remains of Mrs Mary Reeser (1951) found in a blackened circle, "little more than a meter in diameter, a few coiled springs of her armchair, one foot encased in a satin slipper... the skull shrunk to the size of an orange."

Dr Wilton N. Krogman: "This never happens to skulls exposed to usual radiation of intense heat..." Bones have never been known to disappear altogether, no way known burning human tissue can generate such temperatures, what an old priest might croak, "unearthly fire..."

The phenomenon is poltergeist, wilfully defying analysis, once related, by rumour, to excessive stomaching of drink, later to secreted inflammation, a rupture of venomed humours, Dickens' corrupt creature Krook, in a yellowed room, "the air charged with floating soot..."

Gearhart's theory (1975) links the burnings with geo-magnetics, fluctuations in Earth's field, magnetic storms—six cases this century coincide with peaks on those graphs.

MAYBE: maybe EEG patterns, the brain currents are phase-locked to geo-magnetic frequencies or reversals of huge swirled flux, swilled molten core, that sulphurous lodestone belt down there, in the earth body pits, a stomach-churn burns internal organs, solar wind melting in dribbles hisses through cell walls / maybe probability walls sag / in a chundering up of chakras to the bloody flaming lotus / or in geriatrics their etheric body burns out, a hyperthermia, grandmother's ruin, that forces a thin grin, perhaps the whole theme best buried as a small Victorian phobia, like photos of famous masturbators, secret of dirty fire.

Loosening the bowels of analogy there's a fur terror at the happening, scrimmaging words, making heat and viscosity through the body's maze. And yet... If fire burns brown, greyish-black, laws break out, a stochastic inferno. Drizzles of carbon cocoon the seated fireman, why, metric, symmetric molecules of syrup, words are just dripping to describe it.

Brain Gun

Brains grow up
in this domed tank

they swell grand
grand against the scaffold beam
of the usual dimensions

that strong triad
emitted from monad

but then
brains hang in time

over niggling vertigo
this time/that time

that flow
that washes my fingertips away

in vitro
like vitriol

we're maimed numb glossy
as mass roars at energy
through space ahead of us

only hope
to avoid slow death

domed fate
brain dwindling
like nuclear mushroom
in backwards time blast
or crushed in wall of death centrifuge hedonism

apply paranoia to nature!
the phantom attacks!

with brain gun!
the machine!

with grand design
the electrics charge

shrugging through the glia
under dark museum glass
snowing mauve sparks I remember
under dark museum glass

at speed light is/when
consciousness critical fusion speed
fifty per second
mashed harpsichords tingle still

and memory—remember?
serpentine with molecules
wrestles entropy

(so words hit fire burst
30 phonemes per second per second
expansion through
and through)

Half Light

Half-light and snow
the city must look bombed from the air

the star ships are shedding their angel hair
in the half light

and the clock simmers
with cold breath
in the half light

mucous membranes cool off
limbs settle all over the city
in the half light

and this light bulb fuzzes mightily
as if filled with snow flakes
in the half light

in the half light it is always the impersonal present tense

the simple repetition of my used fantasies
would be as boring as the uncrinkling of old newspapers

and the guardian angel is decaying
like a snow woman in the industrial zone

it is uncomfortable kneeling during this ritual of analogy
in the snowy half light
the cows are dying

it is impassible between the cities
in the half light

I'm keeping phlegmatic and husky
in the half light

no good worrying the lady is up to no good
in the half light

wisest to dream of a thudding bass
in the half light

wisest to learn the fingering for a gritty low B flat
in the half light

half light and snow
the city has been wrapped up
like a herd of giant deformed beasts in cold storage

like all throaty adolescents I want my invisibility to be seen by a living
woman

I want certain well-licked phrases to crawl off into the woodwork first
I stand accused of too much fandango in the darkness

I retch like an older man
blindfolded by the half light
the cold glare of absolute iced grit
as thousands of alien white grains
dissolve in the bluish darkness

goodbye dioramas of twilit youth
we plough on wet and cold

in the half light
into the half light
through the half light

                      the light
                      the light
                      the light
                      the light
                      the light
                      the light
                      the light
                      the light
                      the light
                      the light

5

The Slow Ceremony

The Slow Ceremony

1

the slow ceremony
of tasting rubies; lamp-lit
anemones; sea sprite's hair
on fair flesh

lost in a long rhythm
                warm cramps
glee is extended

                to our fingerprints' whorls

in a soft wrench
into glare   creamy flare

and the slow ceremony
                drowning in innocence
the tears flood

so let the lyric meander
trickle of clear spittle on her breast

all fondling of lips
into speech at last

the slow ceremony
igloo'd in pillows   suburban snow

the echo of half-light
fading into brightness

2

a fluency of birds…

        the phantom superior
        LOP LOP
          engraining collaged by blue max

and silverish fluttery

        stutter of ZOOTBIRD

looping the bop loops

"configurations in the interstices of form"
behind the changes
in a chili house near Minton's

labellings

like, KLACTOVEEDOSEDSTENE!

on looping tongue slips/lisps

and twooping

of small/large bird

3

I am not simple; not harmful
but debrained

by information   the mass
of everything timed behind me

the traction/distraction
of her sweetest harsh breath

that deathly whistle: asthma

—if in a random fizzle

    things
            stop

4

Your exam/my invigilation

sunlight shafting

(in my high windowed past
        …its radiant dust in storage
          amphitheatre of memory…)

but now you're asked

what does light code?

and that's the straggle of your hand
across the pages and pages

the questions   wait   question time

is there a substance?

the life and death of the body huddle closer

where there was pain close the gaps

you're seeing (through) it

    seeing it through

5

It must be fed by will. Will keeps it straight, brushes out the old hairy dreams, skin of dulled lusts, scurf of dead hates. Will is total, the peace, her deep breath. That love which shares dirty clothes and finds itself crying, a spontaneous swelling droplet, a rolling wet glitter, a particle of light, that good light.

And why light? An analogue of good? Did we do it, grow a light culture? From our own tissues? The fluster of questions as the lights glow and the sound cues jabber below our window. But she rolls over, wakes helplessly; the day's soon here, with all its clutter. We need cleaning up. Will you? I will.

6

poring over the old slick files
(tonight awash with cars; Cathy asleep)

the cross references… hot wires
behind the sinus… blazing like the floating bridge

man the starry abnormal is in the coming star wars?
parasite rhetoric; erase— just follow the skirl

yes/but (trace the suture) THE COLD FURY
OF HIS MINERAL SPIRITS

AND hold back the twitch
to flick through *Magick* (breathy simper of The
Beast)

to check the Obligations like a holy fool/I
need/imperative
keep a clear distance clean air between the ears

"that deicide (delete)dedication" (don't forget
thoughtful gossip)

"is lethal": a thickening clogged music of pain tones
clustering...

discord: did hooded powers slump
in Sinclair's grey (control) room?

the neons flicker: this talk
massages the dark larvae

yell loud and cold enough
and zombied hoods will cross the car park

to burn flesh-like rubber to turn to bubbling tarmac
and flesh and rubber in a NIGHT OF THE DEMON quickening
remake

RIPPER BOYS RULE—coarse wisp of my
voice grins like irreversible pyorrhea (the demo tape wowing then)

across the abyss /inside/outside darkness: Cathy
breathing in the right places/ there's a light source in human rooms

we know the disease
time's bending, fight the staggers

7

BODY HUMMING/HAMMERING BLOOD BODY HUMMING/
HAMMERING BLOOD BODY HUMMING/HAMMERING
BLOOD BODY HUMMING/HAMMERING BLOOD BODY
HUMMING/HAMMERING BLOOD BODY HUMMING/
HAMMERING BLOOD BODY HUMMING/HAMMERING
BLOOD BODY HUMMING/HAMMERING BLOOD BODY
HUMMING/HAMMERING BLOOD BODY HUMMING/
HAMMERING BLOOD BODY HUMMING/HAMMERING
BLOOD BODY HUMMING/HAMMERING BLOOD

                        blood/light

8

"The profile of your long coat,
cheeky hat"

last night
rigid with conjured need

in dark sheets tents of your absence

left me with an unearthing
I can't grip

        hanging in the dark

for what we have is primary

as the dead night of summer

as stars (dwindling: re-verb each other)

9

Twilight around the lake

stalking green spider forms

an entrance to worlds

around the lake of swords

our enfolding paths

not a neat fallacy

10

the flight low

        across ripples

out of banked darkness

            bird to bird
wakefulness
      in a flutter

glossing magnificent
           this pride

is gleaming transmission through swoop of neck

—and her turning/
    my turnabout

the whole point of alighting

*

"contingent systems" rule and are ruled.

no-one rules; we are lured
into the craft of other's nerves

water vessel/blood vessel
the electrifying currents

that change and change about

*

that inner circling

        out and out

glints

        over silenced waters

11

To have seen the widening swoop and circle of the slowly pulsing bird; to have turned away, on the long run, from the stark instant, a dark minute, in the grass, in fluttering desperation, despair of his release.

All this takes an awkward strength, love.

Later, my poor mate, you were caged, even from the flight of vowels, consonants, breath between the teeth. And below silences, pain is in there, beating.

The bird arcs through free space. He is our speech.

12

our specialised peering and beaking
is agreement:

        pronoun/with/pronoun

murmurs a share
of bed at lights-out

        heater, clutter
        bedroom closes in

at the moment, the moment
is this smaller animal
we've talked ourselves into

breathing out the ice

13

words that are known in the blinded warm room

unchain   unknowing
     crouch over

          silence

whatever perspectives are deranged by rancour

the evolving dormitory of us
animals revolving

that is, a world rescued in blood-
corpuscles of pelican (blood in flood-boats)

turns
     through seven spirals
          into blueberry heaven

(amazing
     radio
          crackles of applause)

14

oxygen nitrogen impurity

disturbed

by nerve electrics

opposite: altarpiece of mirror

a watering place

for optics

mirrored drapes fold

wrinkling by solemn expectation

in high erotics

the two wardrobes

trickle open

sleeping tactics

15

in vocals this foam of the living

opening of frisked blood

in the heart chamber

the shaft of her torso

16

a magnetic song of the three true crows

crosses some palms of a tree outside,

in the little claws of your vulnerable syllables

this morning's contours:

a long fall of light

through orange curtains

17

the naked cleft
opening tree's door

drawing out
the forces

they are not hidden

the naked cleft
the aching exposure posed

is this all/all

(a child is singing in a field)

—flutter by—

the years fill me up
now it is seriously happening

freedom through the skin

witterings of the birds
hornet stuck in the grass

—emerald dragon
  fly opens
    escapement of wing—

the river of feathers

river of lead

the sky is leaping on the planet

18

Sunlight, the richness of grass, sliding water. Those broken noun phrases, lax, disconnected… patterns of massed light, the time dilation, slowing us down, is the shaping need.

The air enters me, her. An apple apparently crumples. Her whispering stops me, talking about Pan? Invisible rolling stock shunts away across the still river, in those trees. Behind, up on the ridge, a car is veering home.

We lie between, in the valley, between these two paths. Self-consciously I hope that the food and the light we're ingesting is driving us higher; but the drift, this dream, stretched on a blue overcoat in the grass, in which we become a glass palace on the water, will grow on, up.

My liquids gloss and lap. She is in the real grass, it is the world. "We want, and we shall have, the beyond in our time…" We are play, free play, like the play of distant voices:

"A trousseau, in which green would predominate, dedicated to Pan…"

The sun sinks, shadows fall, time is humming in its gravity well.

19

"The road to Newton Abbot was waylaid with Red Admirals,
the sky was hot and blue, I walked with the boys to the
bus… every week all that bright vulnerability goes off
into the unknown…"

the mysterious in heart
as romantic as their vanishing points

children are always growing—right out—to the final
blips of the heat of time; on metal heat

they go: and despite bad grammar
the noise of programmed streets won't get them

(at the entrance to that awful playground
the sandpits of adulthood)

and despite the ongoing loss of focus
I bubble with dense memories

*

you made me poet: atomic spy
on the living flutter
of cells "within tiny cells"

and in a small blue-domed room
pierced with starlight
we'll make it new, its small syllables crying

20

What signal is being communicated in the rain? No fancy in the flux of water, these molecules licking through the air, smearing their halo over and all around, to liquidate the syntax of vision in visions—it's all suggestive—"know what I mean?"

In the rain the thing is. The thing is that flutter of water that flattens the rank grass, out there, out front. Like all pleasures in the wet hedges, it's a tiny incandescent thing. You know. All about the rain.

We like the recurrence of rain, the soft pattern, its grey beat. No shame in admitting a preference for tree dwelling "entirely surrounded by water". We're in. It's out.

But that isn't the whole signal. A reading of the rain goes (and grows) well beyond that. The rain states that the swimming of small lights, the

drench of fallen stars, what we fabricate in darts and glances, all that—
and you know what I mean—is, simply, the right forest to pick ferns in.

21

cylinders of silence: a cone of peace
the slowly undulating geometry of sleep

you're crying it out, in slow waves
of any brain's tremor in extremis

but a garble goes on/over the top
all around us the dead beat

of unlistened muzak, its slugging
fibrillation no heart beat

dead dead dead dead
beats a hole in our skulls

and I can just breathe a half-useful warmth of pathos
to right this—all wrong—the deprivation

that all poor are coded into

let's fight to clean/burn

the bubbling shells of that shit neighbourly noise-off
into the silent ground   times flame

or simply the dreams we all need
to slough off yesterday's toxin its dead

22

the dreams consist of curling leaves

in the crush of the latest century

and I'm unbecoming
          so tired, to bed

*

light blows the flesh

our whole weight

needs its rest

so much space

jabs at us

the blackness
above the airwaves

our craft must be ready

in time, time—

23

The spirals of time are now manifest
in the absolute (flesh)

in the unabashed dance of a penguin
in the tableau of limbs the thighs

in the singular placing of fingers on lips
in all the astrolabes, the kissed clocks

the neutrinos ghosting you

24

I wrote in the gaps/dubbed over/these pieces
bits of notation
           and now it must go
all in the rage
of a fear

filling my hemisphere

those manoeuvring plagues the death blocks
you and I and you and I

will wrestle against

all in the urge, bright circuit
of invisible cells mating

through a vision

of parted lips

closed eyes

25

A rabbit in the urban drift
mates against
accumulated dark

           against an edge
red light/dark red

some mating (in)formed
by high time-pressure spun
in the light of recent cells

           we'd go steadily
           to be time burrowers

26

    sines fall; the tympanum is darkened
    by a roll of oxides, through cassette heads

    defences of a secret music unroll

    long memories

            through any/every garden

    of our common speech

    erected in blossoms:

    a tree-hut of the outer suburbs
    where birds queue on the dowel

27

    In a wood near by Bird Kings of the appropriate Sephiroth sing through their elongated golden beaks. These long crooked cries, high stiltings, and flurries through small pools of purified water are methods of proving the existence of their planet.

    The finesse of their multi-layered enamelling—magenta, azure, emerald, gold—fortifies the high mesh of their energies. This is the source of the throbbing magnetism which has been discovered along the curving overgrown banks of woodland cuttings, transmitted along the vibrant narrowing rails, towards that tunnel mouth concealed by bracken.

28

    sky dented with light
    and the foliage of our lungs'
    slow moving knowledge

all that might be fake
a slick zipping of neurons
against swell belches of flame, grit—

but we've become
the eidetic images
that rolled and clung behind our eyes

for the first time
clumsy with reference, careful

29

The slow process

is another helix
of spiralling leaves

the time of years
misty with sparks and apples

and her careful placing of colours
constructs the whole house

to include small and defiant creatures
whose habitat is a sniff of dreaming

and sweet breathing

30

To dart along red runnels
earth clogged quite sweetly
in nails/hard cracks

she needed wider breathing
pads of harebells
various worn stones

between blue flowers existing there/not here
and free-based tranquillity dreams

falls the shadow of many smiles
and the drift of some poppies

31

Field effect: the River Wye. The sun went down, brown. Sheep were on hold. In their droll referendum position. The skein of silence can, be sure of it, a great soother of waters. Stippled water can affect the listening, listing of continuity on the flat mud ooze. You are disappearing down a smooth beach cleft.

I was left behind. Everything was going down so slowly. The drifting dead are all present. All content. I would be. Quite so. The dream lines: The wren has built its bushes and temples in our sleep. The silence of the eel equals the science of a completed tower of dancing glass.

Here we go into a soft wish. The Holy of Days. To slip into the bank, its heaped blood-earth, a subsiding sun. That rabbit is virtually a rabbit to the play of a naked eye.

We went to walk right up into the pig-strewn field. Sheep grazing against the draft of higher air.

The united composition is divided by a jump-jet along the dark jots of horizon, hear this, demon vibrations fantasticated, cockpit death terror, a scythe of smoke, beyond belief.

Grey lion, grey bear, grey mole. Stand near the stones, please.

6

Wapping Rap

Wapping Rap

1. DISCO MIX

these bum notes
means to an end
thinning voices
tenderise and blend:

NO HIDING PLACES
DOWN IN THE HARD-CORE
BELT UP THOSE BRACES
RUB DOWN THE COLD SORES

2. STREET CREDIBILITY

juries of the dead time-courts
pump smooth black phlegm
from all usable pasts into the present
at Maggie's debating society

the grunt of such ranters their factors of multiplication
the flap of their flesh packaging is made porky by emulation
they're opening their veins to close up the streets
"and your preservation of brains under perspex pyramids
is totally irrelevant…"

savagery of the lost classes
craves any tumble from black-glass graces
and on the streets of white stucco
they flypost:

THE RICH WILL DIE

3. DEVELOPMENT AREA

The pylons carry me power; it is the power of mistakes
I am trying to drum out: the pylons crawl across the city,
could buckle in a superflux of light and soon we'll be all plural
a homily of plasma howled through dirt, dance, night

I'm a dabbler, stubbing out words, I frill the forms,
a dingy try to code everything, de-file the torn papers of female wings
while lights crawl across the city some radio is melting

in the deserted oil kingdoms of Texas
Big Daddy triggers shouting match

we'll be alight you fleshers flying/petals/of/metal

4. BENEFITS

everything, too much, over the top, can't stop, rot,
garbage WORLD FINAL SYLLABLE CONTEST
in putter of tinny space

do not wait to see the receptionist
tranny abuses the old smoked men
who cough up for their benefit
sing for dung suppers
in the assigned booths of unwashable oatmeal-plastic

go straight to the waiting room
I try to keep the brain invisible

lacking fibre for the long wait
I use up professional phlegm
but it's ARMWRESTLING! SKINHEAD DWARVES!
until you are called for interview

5. RIVERSIDE

…the old poetry thunders: tugs on the brown river
pull me back to literature and
all of Wapping
was invented in 'The Waste Land'

you can play out memories fast a full rat-squeal of payback
but other noise, beyond browned curtains, signals numbly:
"Bela Lugosi's dead"
at the end of the end
you can squat anywhere.

7

Saxophone Heresies

Saxophone Heresies

Anxious suburban teenager, 1962, eyeing up West End shopfronts, head aches with deep heat beat that won't be put down, his shaky fingers pop as his new breath is smoothly mechanised by immaculate brass riffing, analogue-coded, as curving space-wagons hurtle with glitter and wet perspex off the assembly line into glare, all horny blaring in sex-play of these streets…

These streets scripted with showbiz neon cliché, displaying the horns, in clusters of gold and false silver, plated, sculpted, with flowering gravure, with all the right names—Selmer, Buescher, Conn, Berg Larsen, and the white acrylic Grafton, "as played by Ornette Coleman"—perhaps in the orchestras of sinking ships, as played in the mysteries…

As played in the mysteries of addiction, his addiction to secret names— who played tenor on Buddy Guy's 'First Time I Met the Blues'? And this sacrament of power, the soul that burns beyond the weary algebra of notation, as read by all those light-fingered piano tricksters, faster workers with cool girls, with their orthodoxies of technique, while in the wanderings of his eyes, across the untouchable contours of some distant cheekbone, he knows…

He knows the dark presence inside the statues of the great jazz dead, the self-destructing immortals. He will enter, has entered their darkening infinity, focussed by rays, head-aching searchlights of interrogation/ prowl car/night-train in night rain, which reflects, in swirls of pain, on these Soho pavements. He wants to breathe these night airs, to expel fires, in total voluptuous solid instants of power, a flighting of blackened throat-cries down the hollowing cathedrals of city streets, emptied as the dream of God is interrupted—

2

the horn, uncoiled, tastes dank
useless
dark frayed reed

old verdigris spores
spot the scrollwork

"needs work"

work is scrabbling up a clutter
of staled pearl keys

breathwork is not
pure prana

it becomes him not
these saurian fartz

"up the ladder of Pythagoras we go…"

slow and quack
this little pinko stumbles

up and up
go leaky fingers

trying to try to change old fat-finger
changing brass tube

into horn

"rancid gas maelstrom!"

JABBERWORK ! THE SHAM SHAMAN DRIBBLES!
IT'S THE ID OF THE ME, SHAMFOLKS!

RAMBLE, YOU RABBLE-ROUSER! DESPERADO PHLEGM IS
MORE LIKE IT! RUMBLE THIS TIN BELLY-MAN!
FUMBLES OF PRIMAL WONDER!

WHAT KEY? WHAT KEY!
QUITE LOST IN GROPES AND DRIPPING

BREATHLESS! BLUBBERING! SQUALLING!
AIR! BLURT! GOB! ME! ME! ME!

"try   to read the music."

3

Try to escape myth. Try to actualise it. Try to outrun zoot-suit idols. Try to do the Hucklebuck. Try to control squeaky reed. Try not to nibble mouthpiece, boy. Try to get it off, try to get it on. Try to measure duration. Try to attack precisely, on the dot, liquidly unslur, to full fluency in flight across the semi-tones, and no dirty scrabbling in the cracks, to hear Pythagorean geometries of sound, the clean line

"a tune a day"

and he can't. Must clumsily grope. Backwards. To his root, his false rooting. A half-deaf blabber, this shagged-out, sleep-drenched compulsion to blow. A fuzzy-cheeked pidgin over-blow, to blow, to be blown, right on out!

4

Years later
this customised narration
still replays itself badly

Years later
at the shrine of the blue flame
he mimes his inner riffs
soundlessly

Years later
having hocked all the hooters
when other, more Gothick pasts
spoke right through him,
the dud double-tongued:

Oh God, Oh Baudelaire, Oh bombed-out Europe!

Years later years
of distraction in his secret
secretions of inner ear
the phantom fanzine fancy: to be a foot note in those sleeve notes

Bird/Trane/King Curtis/Ayler

and those midnight mysteriosos
dying like punks

his years of addiction to ghost-tones
must burn off into the night

listen here, now

5

        SAX = FLUTTERING GRIT
    ON BATTERED VOWELS BEFOULED
   `BY INSECT CORES JUICING HOT METALS
         IN CUT FEEL BURN OUT

     KEEP THE HARDMOUTH GRIP
 ON TONE CHAMBER VIBRATION PATTERN
      TO BLEND ALL BRASS AIRS
TUBE DABBED IN BLOOD THAT OLD SPITTOON
            TUNED

    BURST IN A WRIGGLE OF SEQUINS
     IN METAL VOICE HOLARCHY
           FLESH!

6

in a splay of fingering
breaking a wave/waver/wavering
breath

narrowing

to widen throughout the mouth-
piece of starred
bitten metal

through (mucus) into a cone
forced through re-
entrant curves

to the power
of power

take deep-breathing/care

ride the habit of motoring nerves

tickling into click
an heraldic platter of keywork

dis-played

for structure veers back
down to the foundations

above (is below) that level of Malkuth

the titillation of atoms a fiery body mist

there is numerate spirit?
at last/first binary?

sound isn't/is
sono nis

play makes the player
the scuffed elemental of his sighs smoked groans
grows tatty wing-bats buffets
(boxedinchords) vibrant lines vectored/

into pulse beat/flight/beat

fleeing/trilling duration

in the split of time

Miles Totems Up the Homing Pains

(Festival Hall, London, July 1987)

To do the strut around
in peacock lights
green purple

Miles probes
lost touch

flashing twinge of mute

the collective of eros lost

under her breath
at the end of parties
on the beach when she smiles and turns away

from the whole of darkness

its tender gravity of the flesh

in novocaine

The Solar Myth Approach

(for Sun Ra)

SPECTRUM (1.1)

out of local dotted time
through/across
acoustic space
voices of the voidlux
star chamber, star chamber
echo through all colours
the old Pyramidologist, of blackness

REALM OF LIGHTNING (1.2)

a long line scooped from blood red earth jags across baked
ground; but the jungle is walking all its swarm towards
the song, the serene howl, an animal who is rattled and
thundered into fur-throated being, brushing through the
rustling drums

the tatter, the hammer, the pressure, the patter, the fissure
the finger, the batter, the beater, the hitter, the howler,
the scraper, the bleeder, the rustler, the thunder, the
finger, the singer, the thunder, the flasher, the stinger,
the rattler…

the drums tickle, spreading a glint of rainwater across
my favourite bits of you, the drums tickle/a beast/into
glottal yodelling, and light moves in amiable stripes.

THE SATELLITES ARE SINGING (1.3)

the satellites are singing
in hep tones bop tones
across the growl of Harlem tarmac
the galaxies are calling
and we sing this song-pulse
for their great procession

and the syllables are spinning
through solar lofts, aloft and

the steady tread of our joy
trembles in solar cells

LEGEND (2.1)

the rocksichord teetered, telegraphed
some cry from the forest of reeds
a nesting of lost planet reedbirds
who have plaited the nerves of their hives
with stains from brain dance
their story of the chimed rocks
was coming into a speckled light
blazing hole of rock mouths
pray silence for earth's story line
the crystal men and women
just flamed into life
their whole leaping pointillism
was a paint dance energy trace
sound smears for the sun
YHA! through slides of brass
through reddening shifts loops brackets
they drove the verbs chattering at infinite recursions
into the fused-glass columns/doors of star traps
networked, clustered, undecoded/
all creatures glowing up a storm
so many oral transmissions

too much NO radio silence PRAY

this is the story of the living rays

SEEN 3 TOOK 4 (2.2)

THE GREAT CHAIN OF BEING
swings from the sleeping robot

all this is secretly filmed
its great flame of being
sings: the sleeting plateau
all mists; hidden thunder

the crackling solemnities of some great silver beast
framed on slow burning celluloid/to curl smoke
have left us to flutter small new wings

through fluffy rubble
of his great amphitheatre of night

THEY'LL COME BACK (2.3)

their cylinder along the word line world lines
will curve along the centrifuge of light lines
future cabaret along the wiry barbed lines
spinal nova along thinnest scratched red lines

eternal returns please
the stoppage must be unclogged
flow your milk through temporal membranes to melt our habits
please feedback thou hatch owl of the mysterious meat
which is vegetation of unborn egg states

next word is de ja vu
all sticks back like flies
it will be a great ball called experience
it will come like the ecstatic grease of automatic transmission

be a soul train head light around the mountain
out of the laughing red rock mouths
beat the roaring blades
of contracted but undiseased clocks
come back come back come back…

Dead Letter Blues

for VC 1943–1989

His perfect spelling on the best vellum, the last letter.

In that drab flat with the gravel garden.

In the evening, the rainy evening.

In Cathy's quilt, all dusty, perhaps, wrapped around him, hopefully.

"Vincent, you bastard, you've really gone and done it this time," and then she, Jeanie, slim and husky, desperate for fags and sick with a clenched stomach, the furies roaring for real in the wet wind, maybe she howled and kissed his brow.

And I am making patterns with her pain.

And he always played a bit with her pain.

Like he stood up the girls at seventeen.

And he in his satanic pomps gave them points, teeny points for their maidenform tits and having docile personal falsities.

And the dark dark bleak ache on the bald street is really going onwards and upwards.

He used to drone in his madness but at least he went on famously, furiously. "After the Beatles, after the Stones, who else is left? Me…"

I've sat for years on unmade beds listening to all that.

Did I kill him with my righteous summer letter/ Did I kill him with the flying aroma, the flying arrow of my tulpa, the cacking Raven, moulded from his auric excrement?

I wept for the best minds of my generation

too late all the old beat is in the pattern of sunlight across the cold wind, rhythm of clouds across the February sky. They huddle around a greenish grave on the straight and narrow of cypresses while Father John in his biretta with quiet high anglican powers and principalities sprinkles the earth.

To drive out the cockney devils…

O bury the flowers.

Renee peers forward: ashes to ashes…

The day before, poor shaking olive-dark Mizarolli mumbles before the coffin, sprinkles his holy orthodox water with muttered prayers for Vincent's soul.

Vincent is sleeping in his glossy coffin. The candle hisses. He is plasticine in the hands of iron, hands of teak, hands of brass, but he hides his lean feminine gambler's hands

—that played Bad Penny Blues
—that drove the broken english of our
word engines on his screaming Hammond

—that played tricks with spinning dots, and juggled, and carved a chaise longue

—those hands that I broke the spirit out of with my spectral wrath, the ugly syntax of my warped hunchy soul, I must have done, those hands bound away into invisibility underneath the veneers.

He wore a silver-blue smock. A celestial kaftan. With his vampire-proof crosses, he looked very '69, my old hero of sixth-form dances, betrayed by my bland repressions

I was angry with my friend, sayeth the aetheric body of William Blake.

I was angry with my foe, sayeth my bestial husk.

He is husk now, smooth polished husk, his hair in cavalier disarray, his skin lightened by poor brave Jeannie with her emergency pancake make-up and he displays the sardonicus hammerfilm of a smile, smug within the cosy casket, but he isn't here, it has been emptied of brain, and the brain of Crane is drained, but in the snicker snicker cranium his sideways mercurial eyeflicker is going on and on.

He is still going on. He won't stop, the fucker. He walks with his long dog along the high white streets, past the porticos and architraves… maybe the last time… "silly old Vince", he was crying, the stupidest man in the world, as he tried to rail us on to the train at Maida Vale.

On the day of the funeral his dog shat on my shoes. I call that a psychic phenomenon.

He was in the box. I'm certain now. When Michael and I arrived at the undertakers with a last minute floral tribute there was a screwdriver lying on top of the coffin.

Old Tom had just wandered in hands behind his back, clicking his dentures, to inspect the brass plate. As if VC was setting up a small business, a new profession. "Very nice, my dear."

His agony will take years.

And in 1962 VC played his wonderful thunder-god boogies down the phone, the music turned me into a jabbering shaman who embarrassed girls everywhere, but the light fingered trickster at the piano he got them all…

He wore a suit on the summer beaches.

He wore a wild west outfit to my school.

Take it from the top! we yelled.

8

The Slow Learning

Conceived as a "video poem for television"
Directed and edited by Jeremy Welsh

The Slow Learning

Brother Paul welcomes you, not only on behalf of his own sub-personality but as a medium of transmission from a fellow-worker hidden on the sub-atomic planes.

Brother Welsh, like all real—or unreal—sub-atomic particle/wave forms, is acting invisibly, but simultaneously, at a distance, from the Northern Lights. He is not with us. Yet his hyper-reality encompasses us all. He's in the Grey Zone.

His scrying-stone will graze your lips. That's the true crystal text of virtuality. Your truth tablet. Suck the Grey Capsule—and SEE!

This Green wrinkly life-form, a carbon-based mobile continuity device is merely a muttering Dr. John Dee look-alike, wizard of a lost word-hoard, lazar of the library, the monaural magus, the last damned Gutenburg Man, Prospero of the burning books, last of the Hi-Flying Word Men, any mask will do....

I have had my mutations, ladies and gentlemen, I had my intermission riffs. Let's look through the Book of Life. Time was, little sister, when peoples used to call me Little Bruther Saul, the plastic soul man, fifty thousand watts of bad vibrations from the Arctic Circle to the 49th parallel and way on down the West Coast. They called me an all-night worker, a mean green sex machine, a Mekon of mega-funk.

But the old tower of power started to tremble in the midnight hour. A rattle of thermionic valves, the death of analogue. The radio years were blinking on the dial. Even then the future was digital. And The Big Nite of Time, the Night of the Quantum Brother kept closing in, as we speak and whisper together, like the spiders in Nietzsche's doorway.

For I and I, we are being the Quantum Brothers. Our name is legion. We are the polymorph pervoids of the Chaosphere, post-modern, post-production, yesterday's alternate tomorrows postponed and cloned into infinity. We can't mix down.

We stream everywhere, all at once, like demented quarks, under rigorous laboratory conditions. Now you see us, now you don't.

We're the high priests of hype, Hyperion's Bums, Hip-Gnostics of the Rapid Eye Movement, Directors of the Dream Lab, perfect subjects, ideal objects. We're super-cool, the super-conductors, chilled out, but we just keep flowing. Get down, sit down, relax, we do it all, we leap at every opportunity, like this latest ultra-new Campaign for Inter-Active VP—Virtual Poetry, Viral Poetry, the ultimate inter-media product.

We can do it as a lecture series, a corporate training video, a commercial for service industry leisure product, like a new hand-launched heat-seeking ground-to-air missile system, any kind of "public development", lovely job. If it needs sponsorship, we can market it, like beanz meanz artz… This is big serious business. This is control. We must execute.

For you're about to enter a twilight zone—between sub-atomic events in the realm of the cathode-tube and ghostly tremors in the left brain, between microcosmic flutters of the heart and the macrocosmic implosion of stock markets or neutron stars…

Let's profile the mighty theme of human culture itself, and let's foreground the learning process, the learning environment, the slow motion of knowledge that's just about to go fast forward into overwind. Let's critique the status of learning, the processes of aggregating and transmitting knowledge. For the sake of discourse let's go global and and call it education.

We've done the field research, we've had our observer in the terminal zones of the urban education industry for many years, posing as a "supply teacher", who, in lightning strike response to supply/demand of educational labour market (forces) forgoes continuity of role and/or authority of expertise. He hath no presence, ain't nothing but a phantom hound dog, god's piggy in cyberspace. A charmless particle spinning out of control.

Others counsel the curriculum of his daily life. He is the screen where their zany pixels dance, the chamber where the particle-trace of their random fancy fizzes and fades. And the punters know nothing, but they know his munitions ain't smart enough. We just blanked you sir, no body's listening, they've gone into their black holes, their private reality-tunnels, down the subway, down the Tube... We know the principle...

So here we go. Quick, quick, into the Slow Learning. Or visit the Impossibility Exhibition in the Terminal Zones. Jump to it. Go for it. Be what you wannabee. The night time is the right-brain time—a linguistic game show; a private reality test; a dream syllabus; a curriculum counselling session; a meta-linguistic register; a programme for behavioural modification; a sub-vocal lecture; a defensive class strategy; a pedantic weapons system; a learning support project; a course in millennial fin-de-siècle survivalism. An attempt to accelerate into the learning curve...

This is what we learn from TV, TV Me, MTV, as the images settle like sediment, in random access memory, in memory of our dying culture, across the light-years. Join us on the screen of ecstatic refraction.

Supply Servicing

As widening cackles of uncertainty spread
urban graffiti make furry squirms
over the subway underpass

*As the black towers/blocks/towers
riff past the train's sprayed glass*

Blue smelling sparks orgone scribble
drive through nerves' armouring

*As the black towers/blocks/towers
riff past the train's sprayed glass*

Smaragdine table my lost gold
is boxed in time/ "he goes"

*As the black towers/blocks/towers
riff past the train's sprayed glass*

International cubists boogie down space
in search of the perfect money

*As the black towers/blocks/towers
riff past the train's sprayed glass*

Learning systems go to go/go
supply the demand reusable skills

*As the black towers/blocks/towers
riff past the train's sprayed glass*

Pastoral Module

You are the manager of a learning environment.

Learn this: IN TUNDRA HUTS BURN TOO SLOWLY, TONS OF METAL IN THE FLIGHT PATH. I can merge inside her downside, to come up swimming into the pink bedroom.

Bengali boys have provided many layers of deep mix singalong into this homeworld homeworking. Sha Nah Nah Ha. Who's got two red pens?

EATING FUNGUS ISN'T NEW. You can control with little movements, moments of elasticity, YOU SEE NOW, DON'T YOU? SIT DOWN!

Our story begins in the 1960's. The language was tested on animals and human volunteers in the setting of a mechanised factory. That was overwound, so leave it alone. Please listen.
A CLUMP OF HOT ROCKS IS MOVING INTO THE ASTRODOME

Nobody's got a whole sheet on soya or even pulses. WHAT WOULD HAPPEN IF AN ALIEN SOFTLY TONGUES HER TIRED FINGERTIPS? That would be a striking case of non-adjustable role mismanagement. THAT FLUID WOULD NOT CORRECT THIS.

Language Behaviour

The *shout* came out of his mouth with an hairy caterpillar.

This extreme brownness and brothy dessication would have already been closing in on him, despite this omission of the full stop.

He has been working on and in himself for only smallish daily honoraria.

The swollen moon-bum boys with the exactly correct trade-mark appeared in order to shout out of order during his reordering their adrenalin stockpile. They couldn't register his old new age bondage.

He as a reactivated cell mechanism of 1950s-style bourgeoisie was running himself down from the feet up and down to fit them up good in pretty crimes.

The very little silences were painfully hateful, they insisted via direct speech on a shagging aromatic throat-burn.

He filtered them good, he got on with it. It was God all love and working out. If a real object could have forced itself through a share of the community notice wall, a punctuating outcropping hard-on of psycho-membrane, through the chalky greenboard, the grey familial sugar-papa narrative drawings of familial nuclei—that looming agglutinated bulk ectoplasm could have split, spluttered, arterial fluid from the paleolithic lump, the tool of his artefact, to forge their will.

The old syntax cannot deal with the trick cyclists of the third world pulling their long-necked baskets of heroin and neither could he not.

Please, please, please, Sir, rap up a sentence about nuking.

Style Assessment

SIT DOWN SHADDUP YA KNOW WHAT I MEAN
ONE WORD IN MY HAND GONNA CLEAN YOUR SCREEN

GAZUMPING STATUS CHECKS OUT FINE
WHAT'S MINE IS MINE IS MINE IS MINE

FRIGGING IN THE LIGGING AT THE PEEPERAMA
LEISURE SEX IS A BLACK BOX TRAUMA

GOTTA WORD INNABOX BRAINS INNA BAG
GIVEAWAY NECKLACE TAKEWAY SCAG

TAKE IT TO THE BRIDGE
WAIT A MINUTE

TAKE IT TO THE EDGE
WAIT A MINUTE

TAKE IT TO THE BRIDGE
WAIT A MINUTE

TAKE IT TO THE EDGE
WAIT A MINUTE

Lifeskill Management

No use what's a use
crying out loudness
his control is a silicate medium

function: to keep a brisk friction
between the ghost of electrified words
and nudge money

wished he was Jung /YO/ a screaming pope
kids are all younger, Stalinised
into collective dream farming

consuming papers in order 1–10
to be consumed by guileless entropy

Infracurricular

increasing protectionist sentiment in Washington
the only official source of news bright news
more resignations are reported breeze freeze
one of the demands of the rebels teachers believe
speaking of his speech undermine gold scheme
going back on constructive reply on operation
visiting imbalance creating explosion
very harsh produce legislation computer dumping
refugee camp aid mittens "shabby morality"
rejected death penalty aged 67 without going down this road
gold sun boost bomb death pipped the first cuckoo
mainly for pleasure to sow the seeds from a military wing
urgent unrest urgent unrest urgent unrest
the question of deliverability is of no consequence
for the next century had an immoral stance on a technicality
tossed from a passing delivery vehicle priceless antiques
in a designated grey area without going through due process
to face a firing squad stripped in the vicinity of the lay by
to project an image in view of Glasnost policy
we do know she bought an egg we must speak to anybody
bringing new hope for specialist treatment turn over
what is possible in contact provided we can snatch him
with any signed agreement to manufacture the enzyme
for work on thermal imaging to trap victims specially made ones
extra special plant no connection timed to cause maximum death
expert on knots called in on temperature drop to cause injury
in a lake quoting odds on in the world running traffic in death
business explanation is required how it happened
in an independent non-political organisation something very fishy
just as the ploughman begins his digging gas jumped four
gold and gold related generally new highs gyrating
bring back that spark a special kind
well known for its chemicals in the events of recent days

Personal Development

This is an expert system
it is most of you, all of me
but no balls at all
or meaty valves to go loafy

This, in an expert system
signifies higher performances, monkeying
I am not just competent only
I stuff the right noises, right to the right

Inexpert systems
will not sound quite so rich and bright.
I in I can simulate leather stimulus
on stinky clean fingers, you stiffs

systems approach to mammal
or automatic environments
surrounding shunted input
from prettied-up heuristic fleshports

To output larger knowledges
process endless exciting performances

INEVITABLE/UNPUTDOWNABLE INEVITABLE/
UNPUTDOWNABLE INEVITABLE/UNPUTDOWNABLE
INEVITABLE/UNPUTDOWNABLE

Multiple Choice Control

Filling in the boxes
with spittle of quanta: THE BIRD FACTOR

putting a death star
in the right boxes

Play up, ye god, crapping dice
into his lock up box

SCHROEDINGER'S CAT
is darkly familiar

ride a riddim
locked inna box

the random curves
into a plural of new crazies

so try hard to eat the words THOROUGHLY
a new line in distribution.

The Slow Learning

A battle of molecules over the centuries
the precise mathematics of fern development
or a fork in the burning woods.

THE SLOW LEARNING

Decoding the last orders of the brazen head
to change shape very carefully
or a print-out of stellar implosion escape velocity

THE SLOW LEARNING

A more ecological attitude to sex preferences
a declared end to quick lumpy closed-circuit bonking now
or an overwoman's view of the gene-editing suite availability

THE SLOW LEARNING

How the sun is sacrificed to create the order of the biosphere
and electrons fired at TV screens simply turn up at the target;
a supply of ghosts on permanent standby

Learning Centre

wind stopped/the wind-up buildings
falling/into sockets/of enemy craters

"the jewish/hizbollah shackles"
heckle meaning, are hacked

in a roundabout establishment
near wired Cheltenham

via fungi of conical metal
who's in the listening post aha

the fibre sky will tell tales
to assemble hourly

Earth's loiterings
and fancy deaths spreading natter

Centre yourself in the middle of the tone.

The Slow Working

Explain the following, how many and why.
Go on. There is wilding in New Utopia.

Recall the last Oil Fields; entitle these franchises:
LEMMING! MAUREEN! BLOWFLY! ANTHRAX!

the world tube burnt her finger with its intelligence
you have to assert against an age, the unverifiable chrome age

all connections grow in concertos
into a platter of past lives, spin it…

that particular person's lexical radiance
multiplied a terraform for centuries

"that is exactly what the hell you meant"
"try to be nostalgia purified just for me"

his face, her face turned backwards
all for a shortened spiritual discharge

in a museum display: muons, gluons
not those nouns with lights in the midst

the worldly tub steams
with tropological violence

time the motion of a car schematically
too many, maybe 40% surplus, boot up a disaster

in the space to fit our latest work
for tomorrow's commuters in space

he had a further telepathic dream,
called it The Poetics of Face

how air smudged around her legs
her mind remains unsigned

Elsewhere

"Existence is elsewhere." (André Breton)

Poetry is a tricky land. It streams with fluid promises. I have always concentrated on being seduced by it. It becomes also a choking structure, somewhat like the burning lattices of the airy Hindenburg but the printed bluster goes up, who looks for portals in the undersiding of our clones, our cloisterings? We, I mean the terminal users, are taken up into the grey belly of the brain.

Elsewhere is the time-locale. Got to meta-jump that event-trap. So! Constant input of place—exotica hunting in woolly hats, s/o sincere in their Afri-Kars posing with muddied guerillas, mmmnnn, and holidays are too amniotic and dearest.

See Lyn in a wooden house, dished by electrical intrusions from the labs. Fifty years ago my father used to dream of Charlie Chaplin and Ford Sterling. It is all the same, kind of weird, your collectivised molecular activity. America controls parallel space. Where else?

The play of blue. Plural organs are droned and dangled by those tripped events, persons call for the staccato and the finely fibrous and the newly euphuistical. There is a basket of sophisticated marketing in the backing of the frontal lip/in a wisp of photon activity. Try the Baudelairean exotica of sexual decision-making strategies. Vive la différence. Vive le exobiology!

So elsewhere is outside warm trousers, in some sloppy eau-de-nil light in a room, staff only, and I am not in front of my senses, see, répétiteur of a workout on the planes, how bellowing denizens of the higher life memorised all along the watchtowers. Space is on the surface of a very hot funnel. The place to be.

Where Else?

Where else to keep running into, waving one's long pointed head… The House of Youth, where else, as time trap, time share opportunity. Here the fantasy halls of appropriated memory shudder with tramping verbs. Tar traps for tartars, tartan 'n' brass tarts: Somebody's gums at age five nibbled by dragon decay, a fast domestication of fears by the stove. Kneeling in submission to gilt and plaster was a key theme for forecasting punishment. A piece of memory is called a meme.

Don't defer that gratification, try drawing another red crayon aeroplane on broken plaster; but they're never the same again. An infantile patina was once created by secretions and the taste of sugar on buttered bread. That black music box was/is at breaking point. Not enough recorded on spiked drums but the child made many final attempts to rediscover by acts of desperation. I must go on existing in this world somewhere.

Mammaries are not etched in error, terror. The fist boys stop their repression. They no time for it, my man. For them time flies through the morning with a smell of small fuses. It is blue as grass, it is a music of tiny feathers. Peace drills…

There are certain places I will defend, they form my sealed envelope. I am not imitating a shamanic disease. The lamp is an owl in the adjacent sky. Magic should be easier. I am a regret posture. It, the stretched air, goes on for ever against the skyline of stones. The factor miming me is a trick of atoms that were always too weak. So biology should be stronger.

So, for example, he would like to study her icon now, and now. Don't stop there. All the girls are naked in the grave, sir.

Personal & Social Development

fronting the night's mirrors
in search of your latest net stockings

so any exhaustion with beaten wings
tunnels straight into me

I'm already nervous, in the wrong tense
quite flaccid with dread

but I must devise a commercial
without reference to my point-of-sale

for interlocking nightmares
about high security matters

affect/disaffect our raw suburbs
with macrobes/microbes/burnt chips

and no body wants to be joined up
with phosphorescent jottings

the vacant houses are wired
for high consciousness

Preparation

in a private room barricaded with old photos
I'm writing against a grey cold morning/sickness

no buddha plays against the terror
of biting off more than my own head

clarinets march through a radio
to provide local colour

I have not much perception to go on
my continuity is a spiral of invisibility

"in the midst of life we are in crisis
a house is but a shed"

an unfamiliar trickle of pain
is not something to get heated about

everything that lives yells

Empathy Skills

The wind died. The earth split. The fire gave us shit. All those deaths. Disaster master anniversaries. America and Great Britain relate to us. I'll try for upbeat intimacy. So much pressure. *Woomera* was the code for spear.

Bouncing boxes, I'm trying to crack my head open! I'm trying to feel something directly in the middle. But nothing is wha'appen mon, me cyan believe it! He said Canadians, however, like to get drunk and be other people, furtive visitors.

She once pretended to be the skull of the Czar, who lived in another world. The rocket church appeared. To be built of blue steel. I just aggregate stuff for them. The spectators did not have the right tongue of fire for what was happening to them.

They opened them all right up. Up they were tied. I'm trying to get outside the body, you see. Define new orbit. Stick it in amateur night. Trepan me some shamanistics, right, right, voices growing up like smoky mushroom jambalaya. Just shrinking. Cars fell out of the air. Services were abnormal.

The large cities were shown to other planets. Eventually. The world was frivolous. Some harsh additives were really taking the roof off. The world games were desperate. People wearing glasses were shot first. How would you like this new name? He hacked right into the bio market. The names just piled up. It was hard to carve everyone out. There were subsequently ninety minutes of empowered sewage left. The sections crumbled into explosive dust.

Report

the night grows in on you
such is the opening of its electrified tree
and such a tacky cerebellum

optimum privatisation thrills
strike to zip a fart darkly
I tell my comrades

getting too old to opt for demonology
my tag would be perfectly electronic
across the sky-channel

cars whiz as often in comic strips
I want/you find an authentic voice of happiness
high as cumulus and definitely cold

lager depressives have driven through regular
history continues to do nicely
and I wanted to be in it

Departmental Meeting

The chair speaks prior to confusion. The polyglot report makes a good statement. Use is prior to knowledge. Teaching all creatures to talk taller "is" his/her particular bad dream orifice. Stop the stock-pile report piling on the abstract agony.

Don't shout. You are dancing too too lyrically in the sunny spots of his/her own hydrogen/helium street-life confusion. Humane modifications hurt like ears, fingers, toes, all the impatient extremities..

The committee sits somewhere in dry ice. Try to flip-flop their NAND gates, keep your story growing. Plot this: I really "am" supercharged with lost narratisations, trick jargon of very old October letters, smog on a cold lovely cheek, dark calves, it was all as necessary as the higher vacuum of my near future.

He said he wanted pure linguistic targets. They got into the riper flesh of the section. To enrich, to enlarge, to enhance, to expand. A black man in blue denim lived in the wall. Solemn bison-eyes leaves to forage in the south. She asked for quicker identity blips. We demand an ideal drinking system.

She challenged the skills of lying down—such rainbow riots! And don't forget a hieroglyph leaves tooth-marks. He certainly liked the alphabetic bias of the studies but do we whirl our dervishes in this inner room? No, the minutes are all lost on the surface of things. It is a dust rap, dust trap.

Any other business? It was suggested generally the trick is to keep bugging their all-round causality. Don't produce that meaning. She reported back he had an low-profile attitude problem. He replied he was sick of death. They observed a light like molten metal proceeding across the table-tops. She imagined a sun-sign over her bedroom. He filed away her secret teeth. The cupolas of the rockets were suddenly turned skyward, please agree. It will end now.

Options

that boy is missing options
his optics slit/ /nuclear light

but the Koreans have already graduated 21% more
winning the grimace style war

with micro-worlds in space
their video koi will expand a decaying face

into all usable memory
in the economy of time

Throughput

Don't; the pressure; the marbled repression
gas from the back benches
the secret matter of England

the tiny battling Brains of Britain
exchange ripfart rancour

store their Harrovian rules
insist on bowing to piss in champagne buckets

golden showers on her Barbour account
"we mould our lumps and gists by promoting competition between cells"

Current Affairs

I got references, actuality, here, everybody comes, on report. Saddam Hussein went to the desert for a media event in virtual darkness. He cooked yellow liquids in a fuming pot for his guards. They stood in the shadows. He embraced them. They stared coldly over his shoulder into immortality. He nodded in the night, muttering in the firelight, tossing in mystery ingredients.

Now this is real. Insects swerve in the lamplight. Saddam masticates something, a sheep's head perhaps. This is the beginning of Holy War against the games consoles of the infidel west. The suicide squads are off-camera, being prepared for heaven, with its soft fruits and bodies.

The sweet-eating butcher from Takriti is rehearsing to be everybody—technocrat, imam, Kurd, father-figure, good man to do business with. Everywhere he is an artefact. Tonight he is Saladin with a long ladle. Look out.

Reports indicate he is a post-modernist Assyrian architect. His cohorts gleam with bloody stumps. His eyes are constructed as black pebbles. You, madam, could have invented him, with huge reamed tubes and death-rays. We, personally speaking, condoned the interior decoration of torture rooms, what was done to men and women on frequent photo opportunities. He is the preserved djinn unbottled by Goddess Tiamat The Babylon Avant Gardener after some convening of chance wizardry, Nasrudin's bad joke.

Geography

The old motherlands are empty. Scarred hamlets became huddles of burnt shelters for the rest of eternal life. Scorch marks on corrugated iron and the pervasive smell of pus. So much information bleeds in—a woman napalmed in the womb, family-sized torture beds, I'm trying to flatten it.

Go away. You'd like to do it to burglars anyway, why not. Exterminate goolies. Give them the existential thrill, very cheaply. Protect the family circle in the savannah of night, from smell of giant animal turds, the battering of light along the horizon. Fire is falling all over the world.

This violence is the spilled cocaine of history. It make me snuffy, pretentious, puffed up like a tight boil, just to write about it playing with the pound in my pocket, my king-size wedge. How I admired Iago hurling his sword over the battlements, a global gesture, our heroes have filled the worlds with it.

Voice-Over

Poetry's carrier-wave is the over-allusiveness of my times, and the general unfocussed feeling here is that if only we can firm up enough chaos, having it away at a correct signal-to-noise ratio, then some fractal is going to push the globular spaceboat into new shape to save the noosphere...

MY VIEWPOINT IS YOUR VANISHING POINT!

Whatever you like, we can sample it. Please be my victim. There's a current lust for organic material. See today's mothers bubbling under, getting ready to sing along with their choice of acid knickers. The Euro-world of zero pop is post-modern enough for her poultry-sickness love, so they modem it, for instant translation into neuro-vision. Say, she's a real peace commodity fetishist, she'll be shot down neater than a sheriff from the burning prayer towers, you understand what I'm praying? The bulk ego will pump your butt dry.

WE SPECIALISE IN THE INTIMATE EVENT!

The fax remain untransubstantiated. And here we are, frauds of the phatic discourse, in the Kingdom of the Water Goat. Let's stage-manage a leak from the nearest future:

THE VAST MULTITUDE OF GHOSTS ACT IN COLLUSION
SPITTING NEW LIFE INTO ELECTRICITY!

Secret reversed-time communication between those electrons would be the sharp end of orgasm.

WE'RE THE FIRST NAME IN ENTROPY ORGANISATION!

Horus Promo

this boy with a nose job keeps rapping
swing into hi-fi with hot wire-tapping

We heard it through the grapevine

mouth zip up-tight on a dead spliff
I'm extra, fast-forwarding my red/green shift

We heard it through the grapevine

into the hot head-time, bed-time, my pleasure dome
is a leisure centre, just take me home

We heard it through the grapevine

I'm the kind of guy who likes to get around
up over and under the girls dancing on the ground

We heard it through the grapevine

Zero is me, mash up your old mythology
Slash your inner rhythm, I got parapsychology

We heard it through the grapevine

I got a black cat bone I gotta mojo too
I got God this morning, you can eat him too

We heard it through the grapevine

I can learn you from cracking you up to break the code
jack up my soft circuit! I'm in the over-mode…

We heard it through the grapevine

puff to push hollering prophet way out of glitzy coffin
extrude more funky stuff go you boffins!

We heard it through the grapevine…

Leisure Skills

DON'T TURN IT DOWN TURN OFF

she's too anxious his hands are empty claws
the claps fill his ear to create a false wall

DON'T TURN IT DOWN TURN OFF

start-stop, it's only stormy Sunday read my cosmetic lips
please operate on-line management of the red-eye whips

DON'T TURN IT DOWN TURN OFF

any hot little body in the house going to get de-skilled?
play my game with sound-bites let's get killed

Uncertainty Principles

Any person's aphasia. Goes like this. The generating of god-given gaps. My mind is not quite completed. Empty halls for flying in. Cut the log, fog lady. The curl of time and lost interest.

I wish I knew. No sheltering. Out of control, deterioration of command centres. Underlying condition not so green. Uncertainty rallies, into the grey, bubbly with borrowed time against future money.

Less isn't more. That aromatic tarot should have been used more often. Which of the niches fit your archetype? Dreams are out of order. Nasal despair. The nonces fly hither. Base of foggy bottom is a solid rock crunch.

Well I never. The word's decline and fall. The incorrect use of the apostrophe is even more obvious with pseudo-gothic lettering. The waste will be timed precisely. The spectacle failure will under-educate so many embryonic people. That was a mind-control device which failed a test.

There, there. Let us pray with both hands creamy, up and down. The computer has given us verbal superiority, not supremacy. I only wanted to grow new faculties, to fast delicately, to applaud Miss Dainty Nose 1990. I'm quite certain of all that. Quite!

Simulation

YOUR COMPUTER IS ALIVE

the simulated poet virtually replicates
evolving on parallel world-lines

into a Chinese whisper of simians
tuned into different fantasies

at a first sighting of dead microphones
splitting new life into electricity

the universe only contains one electron
evolving on parallel world lines

the stimulated poet loses it loses his verb,
to increase productivity modem it

for instant translation into neuro-vision
steal his word (world)

for our universe is scattered backwards in time
the sky is used for a tattoo of interfering signals

BUT IT'S DYING

to increase productivity
 multiplex vast multitudes of ghosts in collusion

Homework

You just try to improve my improvisation against death. Its loopy memories were suppositories of the wise. The sentimental learning is to forget a secret, slow burn of child heat. We braves, tied to our separate trees, sizzle quietly on the big set…

I can see clearly now, kilometres of sand, beach huts in the rain. Enclosures of shame, for initiates only. The rhetoricians cannot eat their prizes. I can see clearly, now, that virtual poetry is a disease. War of the hidden god on the human brain-operating theatre, tinkle of autoclave—why is the world just so terribly quiet—why is this global labour of killing a few scruff birds tagged as friendly fire.

A bitmapping of the smart world keeps our boys going mad in the sands of some condom-strewn desert. They're not sartorial now, no. Their refined squashed saurian remnants won't be worth a squabble no use telling that to the blotto planet. Memorise another dream of blotched flesh.

The plebs wanted their eating contests their three-tier fucking displays to explode a blot in his lobe. I am some thing in itself, an object of tissue on the surface of the earth. A little machine ticks. That is how the last three hundred years had been writing itself, with a little ticker. There's a smell of old factories in the sky.

"They hung the flag at half mast in front of the ink and paint plant. It's all gone, all Sikh shops now. Went out last week, round the corner for chips and brown ale and got mugged of all the weekend shopping. Terrible about that bunker full of petrol. Went to hell and back."

The Korean neighbours' children moo in the summer garden twilight. The world goes on telling its story of willies and worms: a beginning and an end, in blurts. I was a tiny creeping thing in the holy places, the white fortresses of Old Europe.

Overlooking the suburban privets and sycamores, the despoiled Groves, I carefully fantasise about more neighbours, the drunk office workers, high on pain and repetitive stress, hunched over work-stations/war-stations killing each other with high-velocity steel pellets and complex petroleum distillates. They have been on special courses and will have to take work home.

Droplets of water fall into the garden. The tree advances on the brain of the house. This brain joke has fired back at us. I would be far more comfortable with a context/without a cortex. That's full strength sick humour, see.

I don't know. I just don't know. So many activities with bottles and pills and trolleys. Moving houses. Always moving houses. And we constantly try to re-draw the mental map. The sheep won't wander. Corridors of the pre-war consensus. "It was a safe time". Stiff but safe. I collect these soundsnaps as I go. "As long as we know." The phrases that repeat themselves are the only flags of convenience left.

A human dying at the end of the century, fin de siècle, dying amid home comforts, all mod. cons, and the imagery of Nostradamus. The century is slowly folding in on itself. So her neurochemicals are duplicating out of symmetry, a tiny, tiny change, "cell by tiny cell," the Gioconda of Pater's Renaissance, all out of sequence. I'm tired. Watch that anagram shiver with exhaustion. We tried, we really tried.

9
Brother Paul's Blues

BP Blues

Welcome to my car boot of fictions
under the old brown sun

every day I have the news

and the colourisation of our pomps
is a twenty/twenty intromission woofer
or ray-traced micro-drama
to keep the markets puffing like mambas

After the break
the conical descent into dreams
into pealing farce
a collapsing lung of laughter

The gravity sucks
It is our sucker
It is the sweetness of flies

This reporter is hot wired for dissolution
no central metaphor
only webbed right out
into the fatness of spiders

but a pipette of birds
signals through angst routines
street lamps are not quite yellow

—the neurons jump ahead of me
as I fall through this world—

Mammalian cock-ups
guide the cursor

gradients of time trip the alarm
sound dies in the muddied garden

blue cutaway of the sky
was a useful construct
stick yourself into the world
don't take the Kabbalah to heart

The machines living on/in
my nano-memoires of noir
are a mere jungle of dendrites, that's me

But the mummy of memory
makes it all better
in this commune of bombardiering

Bussed in past the Hate Bars
and the hottest green neon flicks
or locked onto cells of messaging

I/we/you/they/the whoever
driven by the hotter pedals of marketeering
career parabolics here we go

Data-mining himbos to sell body armour
the generals are generalising their genre
and playing with our genitals yikes

Sky flattens us all
with ludic clouds
beware the iron bollock descending…

Urban

urban blues mapped my suburban life
strut that street white boy
making the mojo news
beat faster in the burnt-out heart

city of takeaway indians sourced with additional dialogue
login logout you menu mouses
text of bricked up windows and broken English
reads in a triple-tongueing over fiery abscess

as news read by winkers against the blankness of rainy cathodes
how my old beta-tested friends the black towers slide like clouds
all those creations sliding into black furry tunnels
nubiles with their mobiles

fighting the play-dirt with papery marketing flutters
a software infection zapping the corridor of mysteries
lads just tie a mannequin round their heads
and addle addle through canyons of long junglist concrete

pumping the buttburst of their metallic wheeled tombs
their tires moaned of raw whores
explored this fun module for today's living in collapsed spaces
now I don't take any fat tubes of pus for an answer

the city has been installed for plug'n'play mode
ha ha for the the glitches
now continuum city has no end but the burning edge
onwards and outwards in a black snowburst

ad-busted leisure zones flash forward
every stretch of limo
pity the imploders and the ouija squeegees
squish the machines through the glass ceiling

wonder boy how he makes a dollar
just enough for the city

that neon amoeba
sleaze me, sleaze me, mellow baby

to reverse the spin on my molecules
slimming my old time-line
slam into your tremolo wavelength

don't quit your sinning for me
his teeth must have been numinous
gig gig those bytes yah

the streets corral multipedes of fast shoppers
don't forget to set your mandibles
to suck the gritty wind

an artist packaged to go wants spare change
maybe the rich will die in smoke

scribes of the city co-wrote their sentences
in chopped lines of protein

Seething Vacuum Data

1. DRAFT

mix down the prisoners of a memory module
territorial quarks vector them on, on
into the, these lethal sand-castles

we dig amino acid clean-cut
hey clouds flushed out
o'fun with patriotic fire

rhetoric eases a marching order, is,
love me, love my death,
what you initiate.

the earth was still fully conscious
the mother of battles
screamed full face in camera

SCUD: pay respects to a beached shark
today's greatness a flaccid steaming penis ho
stick with that mothering turkey hear me

fire snorting its rocks off
crawls across some raggy geography
to say something neat

2. DATABASE UK

ruins of powder mills
stone needles, clear brown water
ripples under cloud cover,

tourists for ever await
themes arising, deaf music,
a slow flight into bunkerage.

start revision of hissing mystery,
the factoids, I can't sit down,
to rebuild a Sunday shelter, sir, bloody words,

won't code, too much laughter at their edges,
never enough bums on seats to stop the brain in the drain,
drive carefully through the pillage.

3. STATEMENT

He has been statemented. "They entered a religious facility." This is more mortgaged language. There is a hidden connection with Young America. Simulation of purchasing power. Group mind living in eternity via sound bites.

Simulation of purchasing power via hi definition sound bites. Inertial guidance. These inaudible children are buying imaginary houses. The Brits sit around a talking table that murmurs of mortgages, everyone stands up on the wrong cue.

The helicopters play at bitch salvage, with the coo-eyed kittens of bleached fur. Hot blood for a young epidermis. You can't misread the signals. Water towers are the focus of desert prayer. Politically corrective juices will burn out the dead white males.

Find the loop before the beat closes in. Here's an old man cruising over the deadline, far far away. So bite that beat up, chopper some hot meat!

Inertial guidance. The secret War—for a game show. The surprise of suffering. The silverfoiled baby milk factor was faked. The war grew out of an old dream he had, like a pot plant in time-lapse. Listen to my loop now. Bite that beat. I am too flattened, facile too. Colanders, woks, domestic implements—an adventure in metal. Habitual liars glided into limos. Stretch their limbs, easy. They had been in and out of so many hotels that they had developed a new form of amnesia.

4. WORK STATIONS

a cat leaps forward, between the new kaons,
an uncomfortable place within physics:
non-locality is a condition

other entities are widely separated somehow
to be contacted
as imagined, chestnut highlights on hair, no more

oh heads of vocative texture
I don't wannabee centred
on a signing point: I have done no work, no shopping

unearned income: an unpleasantry
while the peasants tore her dog apart with their bare teeth
Gilbert and George were lacking a newer refrigerator

tissue is the issue: I is a live sample,
please get out of your regular body
into a three-body problem, darkly

tyranny will be pro-active,
to register the next of kin
in appropriate symmetrical buildings

I become a useful jelly of time, really
as my centre hardens
a mighty sententia, sir

a red spot in Jupiter
keeps steady as she goes bump
I want to be fascinated by spooky action

her groove thang could be (well) posed for altarboys
I go, I come, tic, tic, tic, tic,
munching an iceberg

the friendly bodies of unnameable meats
slowly unlearn, unravel their spiral bouquets,
as the bonds rip such mimsy memes

I tried getting straight out of my body into a real persona
twanging the cultural channels,
to wander through a world for the sheer ruin of it.

5. ADDRESS

a boy paces his garden, invoicing discontents,
he can't help himself
to be innocent, the serpent,

an aeroplane full of plunging Catholics
was thrust down, down, they shouted like hoarse mammals,
during his factual dreams

he devises a completed psychology
for the pools of theme-parks,
packing in those latencies, frequencies, the splash-paradigm!

this tree is used stick-wise
to beat the wind
can you imagine bare legs with difficult movements

the syntax done broke down
the qualifiers have failed to locate us in space/time
throw out your bouncing voices

he says we do not know
what light really is
search and replace the nights quickly

the omni qwerty board
and screed of grey biscuit
is not yet a real good

biology is successful repetition, almost
and now a break down is a break up and out
from the aggregate volcano mix

keep driving into the nearest silence
I'd like to shoot more people for spitting
the capital smells of black-out

the culture of the bank was criminal
but divided into sectors
in a delicate thought experiment

the observer is suspended between life and death
in a condition critically tested inside many homes
while spangles go blittering at all hours of day and night

6. SURVEY

the perusal of an empty kingdom
will be backed by plunging guitars
nevertheless the flugel of last night blows strongly.

the district is built up around me,
a shiver on a bit of old road, sire,
no way out, but you can't get into dreamtime,

that limited company of gods whose shadowy tubas
control the holistic territory
I would like the sky to slide open please

don't go on shopping, for ripe bile, horse oil,
what the feeders beep
as a sacred shitload of sheds

try to excavate the underlying physics of this
has to be a real lug somewhere to tug
open the inverted flower of a large sky

underneath the arches a musty tramp
bounces his skull with assistance
his swallowed runes say you will get somewhere

this is the pretty beyond
oh that I am burning dust
to shut your mouth with coincidence

broca's area would disgust me in person
to escape the lump you must
not stay here with the stupefying tunes

Dump Cracking

Could quite easily refer to some form of damage that needs to be dumped. Describes the process of diagnosing faults in programs of system management software.

Seek a future role in post-mortem dump-cracking, to check whether a failure was caused perhaps by some incident long ago

1

how a mind works out
at a flame-grilled edge of tonight

how phenomena turn tricksy
no longer in a safe middling
where cubes of wise books talked gravitas

humming roomscape presses it right up
against a glaze of being

2

the sky the infinite hole

tools useless in the wide wind

perforations of time

to burn your garden furniture

the stars hiss down

unshielded radiance

3

The voices of the war crowd in. Heads push up through the sands of many dreams, spouting blood. This is the sport of kings. The heads swivel as they scream. But who has buried them? Is this the timed homework of our homeland? Is it a general issue pack I must vomit up like a bolus of demonised pork?

4

a descendant places the old word
in his new mouth
tests it for plosive impact
giggles carefully
dropping it into the syntax
and picks up a plastic brick

5

Man with breadfruit tummy (fur-covered) sits across pink bed. Hope his signs will pull him into being-in-itself. He's sick with vagueness. Real people are out there building dams, guns, machine tools. They have hot essence.

6

I enter myself in the frame
of apocalypse comix splatcake
dancing in the brilliant squares

recall father nodding at death
and the house sinking in the mist
children save this time capsule

Bad Memes

1. Solar flares bake the entire people

Such articles generate
saliva and acid
such are the humours of the pink meat

At the end of the day
I under-compressed myself

(such lost flashes of signature
remembering old trains
like bombs asleep)

while transpersonal wavelengths
cornered the market

eyeballing our mosaic
the hegemons of glitz
humvee down the tepidarium
to pork those pecs
now you have peak dino-porn
a completist action plan

2. Problems with signal flow

All liquefied with dreaming, he walked down the wide village street. Her fingers clutched his head, or perhaps a hand. The shops were antiquated. They peered into a bookshop, with a red plush haute couture section at the rear. An old woman in a mantilla was being denied access to the fashion section. The plump grey beardy owners refused her card. Anyway, he could see a copy of a very rare book by Mike Horovitz on a green baize table. It was superbly illustrated with industrial prints by Eduardo Paolozzi and cost seventy pounds. He couldn't afford it but said he'd be back.

3. 60-second man

Can't talk the walk
I'm such an infested host

4. The Dreams keep feeding backwards

The landscape was always the same. Within seconds he could see the golden blossoms crowning (crowding?) the great Winged Mountain. The entire hillside was beating with horned hairless wings. There was much noisy throbbing of membranes. Each wing, planted at random in the dusty rock, was at least two metres in height. He found the repetitive beats comforting. He was well into the deep structure of something, or someone.

Halo

Holy war. A rolling war covering the holes and orifices. The war is submission. They get off on it, over it, over us all. The boys will piss in the deep graves as instructed. Crawl off to the sewer that has been reconstructed by the servants you have forgotten about. Who will save the hot babes in the bowels of the earth and all its hospitality suites?

My sentences can't compete with the screamers. The prayer towers were predicted. Their wheels and rays increased the harvest. The blue screens of Earth flickered.

Halo of heat. Dirt in their wounds. The uncovered head glaring. Night waves. I can't stop blogging it. Sleeping apart during the gloom. For cool's sake. A queasiness of being. Stop the images.

Bus gut and the tubular coffin of granulated fire. And the woman who lost all her limbs, rolling. That's faith for you. Mystery bag man, rummaging and muttering his agit-prayer. He is replaceable kit.

I'm writing a mediated script. I'm a conscripted mediator. With an advantage of remote control. The liquefied moment of exposed organs and the scream that comes out of the chest like a special effect. You can't believe it's you.

Helpline is a deadline. The down line is dead. Trudge on the dead rails. No looking. Just don't stop.

Brother 13

I come in peace
to Lazarus Point
to save the old souls

The granite split over millions of years. The water mass attacks the land mass. The rocks are flattened into stone tables. Landing sites. An altar for the brutal people?

I come in peace
to Lazarus Point
to save my old soul

A presence in the standing firs is stalking the seniors in their cabins. They fought the darkness and the swooping eagles. Now there are lights at the cross roads. The guides speak ill of this place.

I come in peace
to Lazarus Point
to save those old souls

"Lights in the wood…" All old Norm remembers. Guys from the university came up in a float plane. "Ask him about the stalking…" But he wouldn't talk any more. The dead trees talk. They tell the same old story. The clearing in the firs. The burnt circle.

I came as Brother Thirteen
towards Lazarus Point
to save the lost planet

In the glades the light split right open. You could walk right into it. I could be stalking the Sister in the burning circle. I could bring it on down, down, to save the lost souls buried in the trailer park, the tattooed girls in the art bar, the lost fishers of the white crab god, as the rocks collapse around them and light splits through the granite.

I come again and again
into Lazarus Point
saving the lost sister

AJKG 1915–2002

The gravity of money—"sordid finance"
pulls him down into his cardigan
and the easeful chair of death
and its deep breathings

Tried to sustain the long time-line
bringing books to keep the past flickering
the engravings of old circumstances
that were once all-coloured

Brighton 1936 young bodies on the surging pebbles
the roaring forties in khaki his latinate syntax
imposing order on the chores of his corps

We kept trying to reconstruct him
as a scaffold for ourselves
he was brave to become an archive

Bulletins

The rain bulletins open a wound
it's sticky in the comfort zone

In the desolate aisles I/we runabout foraging
sizzled by brands

All colours bleed and run
in the soaped world

Vodcasts target the dread of dreams
re the decay of breath, bad follicles

The subject sits sideways like an object
distracted by rival cars

Who is the feebled verb
In the amphitheatre of coloured rhetoric?

Let's love a cone of light and music
an opening in the atmosphere

Brain Stems

Sleeping on the dangerous planet
to discharge the daily toxins
and ghost a new narrative

Into the fuzz, dream janglings
won't shut up or down
in the forsaken lavatories of embarrassment

but the senses are a front
frontal or fractal our humint
is a conjugation of weakling verbs by night
desire flares into fuzzy logic

the time-ship is only a time-slip
shadow time compresses the decades
into sagging pyramids

the royal we lived through vanishing decades
clotted with the side-FX of music

the tickling duration
per annus mirabilis

the mould of sensation
the serrated tongues of memoir noir

and solid gold qualia
like her cool rump in a rooming house
walks through the night with violin cases
or chattering teeth
haunted by birds.

Thanatron

We're channelling through the Thanatron. We're watching. Watching with care. Yes, we have been observing your observations for quite some time.

We kept our distance in the dusty corners just outside the cone of light, on those long nights as you struggled at your desk with the equations, scribbling over and over those first proofs of survival.

We heard your bitter murmurs in the lab as you struggled on, unfunded, with circuit boards salvaged from surplus stores, cannibalised oscillators and capacitors, cathode ray tubes from thrift-shop televisions.

We watched with you hour after hour as you stared into that array of screens, into the blizzards of dancing pixels, headphones clamped tight as the white noise raged, listening and looking for the waveforms of life.

Life forms. Life forces. The ultimate in pattern recognition. Life beyond death.

You've been dreaming of this for years. Yes, we know those dreams. You dreamed of one deceased, calm on an autumn park bench then turning away into the mist.

"I must go now…"

You dreamed of her quite young, short skirt, bare legs, giggly, pushing an iron bed-train that fills the whole street as the moon leers down and spiky wings break through the tarmac to enfold all things. You dreamed of Eros and Thanatos. Hardly surprising.

And/or you dreamed, over and over, the slow inevitable fall of a long silver plane into wasteland, to burst silently in a blob of fire. We were indeed watching.

And we're all here now as you lean over this flickering display, your familiar jaw and cheekbones highlighted by our pallid green radiance. Adjust the Thanatron with care. There is much to learn from our side.

As we radiate. And multiply.

The Thanatron fades and fluxes. When channelling is initiated, never disconnect.

You asked about the gardens on the other side. There are an infinity of gardens, here and there. Your childhood garden where you stumbled on a rusty sundial and tore a ligament. Another garden where the skull cracked and you never walked again. A garden of high rank grass, concealing a stone. A garden where she smiled through the leaves and called your name. A garden of cracked baked earth. We know them all. Now. In real time. Or times.

Beware of the dreams. Some of us believe they are dangerous leakages of alternate life-content, coded, repressed, noise-infested. Others postulate they are random noise created by the incessant bifurcation of world-lines, accessed at the quantum level in neural networks. But such dreams are not prophetic. Be assured of that.

You keep enquiring about our After-Life. We can see you fine-tuning the controls of the Thanatron, as if our collective blur was almost a disappointment. Where are the hierarchies of fiery angels good for all eternity? Where are the wise spirit doctors? Or the sprites who play japes with tunes in the darkness? And where are the lost parents, the deep warm hum of ancestral voices, the great Old Ones, where are the survivors? Where are the opalescent corridors into deep-time?

No rainbow perspectives. Only the greenish-grey glare of the Thanatron receiving our channel. Your channel.

Look hard. Concentrate on the screen. Reflect and compare our garbled reflections. Trace that familiar beaked nose, slight recession of the jaw, our collectively selfish genes multiplying into an infinity of presences. We're infinitely present. In you. Present tense. Streaming and split-screening.

All the worlds are open, sir. Just the screen of the Thanatron separating us. All going entropic at the same rate. Sorry we're all going down slow, together. No post-life. Only alt-life.

We must go now.

Acknowledgements

Books
Basement Mix (Galloping Dog 1985)
The Slow Ceremony (Spectacular Diseases 1985)
The Slow Learning (Institute for Random Studies 1991)

Anthologies
Contemporary Poetry of British Columbia (Sono Nis, 1972); *Inventing the Future* (Bellhaven House, 1973); *Angels of Fire* (Chatto, 1986); *Words We Call Home* (University of British Columbia Press, 1991)

Magazines
Angels of Fire; Chock; The Echo Room; First Offence; Folded Sheets; Grapevine; Karaki; Kudos; Label; Little Word Machine; Loot; Mar; Negative Entropy; New Worlds; Not Poetry; Oasis; Ostinato; Peeping Tom; The Poetry Buzz; Poetics Journal; Poetry Review; Prism International; Ragtime; Reality Studios; Split Screen; South West Review; Stage One; Suenos; Sunfish; Swot; Synthesis; Tangent; The Terminal Journal; Third Eye; Ubyssey.

Radio & Audio
CBC Anthology: CBC Ideas; CBC Stereo Stories from Canada; CYVR Writers in Action; DNA Audio Magazine; Sound System Man; Reverb; Pacifica Radio Network; WFMU-FM; Resonance FM; Culture Court CD

Web & On-Line Audio/Video
www.culturecourt.com
www.greatworks.org.uk
www.blazevox.org
www.shadowtrain.com
www.cafeirreal.com
Radio QBSaul
qbsaul.blogspot.com
www.toxicpoetry.com

www.ingramcontent.com/pod-product-compliance
Lightning Source LLC
Chambersburg PA
CBHW022011160426
43197CB00007B/385